Be the Bird

How to Avoid the $1+ Trillion "Wealth Management" Shakedown and *Protect & Enjoy* Your Assets for Life

Bradley Clark, CFP®, RICP®

An overeducated nerd in New Hampshire who lost it all—*and got most of it back*

Be the Bird
Copyright 2023 by Bradley Clark
All rights reserved

ISBN: 9798218098797
Printed in the United States

Contact the author at: bradley@bradleyclark.com

Dedication

In honor of the late, great John Clifton Bogle (1929 – 2019), founder of The Vanguard Group, who inspired me to think bigger.

Table of Contents

Be the Bird

Foreword

I first laid eyes on Brad Clark in May 2002, or maybe it was 2003.

The years run together when your livelihood depends on chasing investor "eyeballs" and courting fly-by-night dot-com advertisers, all while enduring the antics of the global financial markets—especially years like those.

Our reputations preceded us both.

He had a right to be cocky: prep school, Harvard undergrad, Stanford MBA. And I had a right to be dubious. I was a public-school kid, but even then I'd encountered enough bullshittery to have a nose for it—and I'd heard his song and dance before.

More than anything that morning, I was hungover and in no mood. To my right and to my left and mostly to my front slouched a skeleton crew of misspent youths: the few dozen or so survivors of a dot-com smashup you could only describe as glorious.

They'd been taken on board it seemed like yesterday—by the hundreds—in a rush of reckless valuations and stupid venture capital. They hung on now by virtue of voluntary pay cuts, merciless bank debt, and the largesse of company founders and their families.

Mostly, they were hungover too—mainly from the night before, but also from the harrowing journey of the prior half-decade. You could say they'd earned it.

And to be fair, we'd learned a few things by that late spring/early summer morning, whatever year it was. You could, by and large, mistake some of us for proper professionals, if not actual businessmen and -women. We were even making money.

Yet there we were again with the wolves at the door. Frankly, it was getting old. Or so I ruminated as we stumbled into Day Two of Foolapalooza, The Motley Fool's once notorious, always raucous, and quite possibly final three-day annual corporate offsite.

Brad Clark, for his part, was downright chipper. He might literally have whistled a tune as he ascended the makeshift platform at the front of the conference room, smiling in his Brooks Brothers khakis and his blue-and-white striped shirt with its separate white collar.

Nobody noticed. The few eyes that were open that morning were transfixed by a truly hideous PowerPoint slide that towered behind and slightly to the right of our dapper young hero. You couldn't look away.

I didn't know what it was, and I didn't much care. But it sure wasn't helping. Frankly, it looked like I felt. Just then, with a flourish, our brand-new hire and latest corporate savior flashed a hand at the spectacle behind him and introduced himself with this:

"I don't know what that is, but it sure is ugly."

Of course, he knew exactly what it was. That hideous masterpiece, with its "pictures and arrows and a paragraph on the back explaining each one," was nothing more or less than Bradley Clark, MBA, thinking BIG.

I should have known.

Only a big thinker could have conceived such an abomination, much less have produced it... somehow bending Microsoft Power-Point to his will... and then decided to project it in all its glory on a dank conference room wall in a room full of total strangers.

To say nothing of realizing the absolute and utter absurdity of it all—and having the social grace and self-awareness to admit (dare I say boast) as much. Little did I know then, that wouldn't be the last time Brad Clark beat me to the punch.

What it was, more specifically, was a graphical representation of our quirky financial website's lead generation, content marketing, and new member conversion funnel. Or maybe I should say, what would one day be our lead gen, content marketing, and new member conversion funnel.

You see, at that point, much like the entire "commercial" side of the Motley Fool business, that hideous graphical "roadmap" was largely aspirational. In a few short years, it would double our free cash flow and do it again (nearly five times over) on four times the revenue. More important, it would spawn a take-no-prisoners culture of disruption, testing, and data-driven marketing that would shake up the industry.

In the 15 or so years that followed, its legacy would transform an unfocused, cash-burning, painfully cyclical, ad-dependent virtual "not-for-profit" with an uncanny aversion to asking its loyal customers for money into...

- A thriving, uncommonly sticky, seemingly recession-proof, subscription investment "advice" business with half a million paying members on three continents

- A diversified, multi-disciplinary workforce of more than 500 full-time tech, creative, marketing, investment, and management professionals, and part-time contractors worldwide

- Annual cash revenues, though not public, reasonably estimated to be in the hundreds of millions

Again, Brad Clark wasn't the only smart guy in that room that late spring/early summer morning. We were already a creative, reasonably tech-savvy group with visionary, charismatic founders, a few mercenary bean counters, and a small handful of legitimate management types.

Seriously, by virtue of having survived the dot-com crash, we had a right to hold our heads up. Nor do I doubt for a minute that many more, even smarter folks joined that crew in the years that followed—both before and after Brad Clark moved on.

But you can believe me when I assure you: I'm not the only one who would privately acknowledge that it all started that morning, in late May 2002 or 2003, with the arrival of Brad Clark and his hideous PowerPoint slide. Much as it pains me to this day to say it.

You may have noticed...

I have little interest in selling you on the Big Idea of "wealth management," or "retirement planning," or even the big ideas you'll read about in this book (though with decades of professional investment experience myself, I can vouch for them without a qualm).

I've been around long enough to know that not everyone needs their wealth managed or their retirement planned. At least, not in the conventional sense you hear about in the financial media—or worse, from the trillion-dollar "financial advice" marketing machine.

Quite the contrary, as Brad will tell you himself, more than a handful of individual investors can navigate the entire arduous process on their own. You may be one of them. But the fact that you're reading these words right now makes you a hard read.

On the one hand, you could have sought out one of the more, let's say, mass-market "retirement" books out there. I won't name names, but the fact that you're reading Brad Clark instead of those folks inclines me to believe you are frankly smarter, or at least more analytical, than most.

Meaning, of course, you probably could handle this on your own. Assuming you have the time and inclination. On the other hand, you wouldn't be reading this book if you didn't at least suspect there are more sophisticated, off-the-beaten-path ideas out there—or that you might benefit from a little extra help.

Whatever brings you here today, you've come to the right place. In the next few chapters, you're going to encounter a surprising number of concepts and strategies, ranging from the outright arcane to the deceptively commonsensical. Including a few simple "tips and tricks" that can literally change your life.

You'll also learn a few things you might not know about the sorry, predatory state of the U.S. financial services industry—plus how much it can cost you personally and the steps you can take to protect yourself. Finally, you'll meet and get to know a rather unusual—I might even say weird—dude.

After all, this is much more than a book about retirement planning. It's a book about money, about wealth, and about discipline—even about life. I can guarantee you'll learn stuff you didn't know. Most important, at least in my experience, you'll see familiar things in slightly different ways that make a difference.

Of course, what you do with all this is up to you. If you're like me, you'll put it to use plotting your own course. If, on the other hand, you've got a real job, a tolerable family, a life, you might simply share what you discover with your advisor (or better, stash it in your back pocket to keep your advisor honest when the time comes).

Or maybe you'll reach out to the man himself and learn more about Brad's unique approach to helping high-achievers and aspiring retirees realize their own vision of retirement, free of the compensation and agency conflicts that plague so much of the financial planning industry.

Whatever path you choose, I can assure you of one more thing: if anybody can take a discipline as tired and picked over as "retirement planning," dig deeper into the weeds, put a fresh, new spin on it, and show it back to you in a whole new light, it's my old colleague and friend Brad Clark.

Listen, I don't blame you if you're on the fence about all my nonsense. When I first laid eyes on Brad Clark, in late May 2002 or 2003, I did not want—much less think I *needed*—his help. Our little ragtag outfit had battled together, and we had survived. And remember, I'd been around.

I'd done a nationally syndicated column, and another for the premium arm of TheStreet.com. I'd been an analyst at First Call/IBES, operated by the world's top brokers, and what's now Thomson Reuters. Wall Street's buy side paid thousands a month for our data and another thousand or so just for my team's research.

In the past few months, I'd helped Motley Fool co-founders David and Tom Gardner launch their flagship investment advisory, with a second, more exciting service on the way. The last thing I needed was some Ivy League spread-sheeter with BIG IDEAS telling me my business.

Frankly, I thought we had the right stuff right there in that room that morning and could handle our business in-house. On this last point, I may have been right. But on all other points, I couldn't have been more wrong. Sometimes it pays to know what you don't know.

A decade or so later, when I heard Brad Clark was toying with "wealth management" and "retirement planning," I had to see it for myself. The whole idea didn't strike me as, well, challenging enough for that guy. I flew up to New Hampshire—of all places—and found a changed man.

It was the same story all over again, though with a twist. I assumed Brad Clark would put a new spin on a concept I always found cold, if not downright dubious, but who could have guessed it would be a more human spin? I won't spill the beans here, but let's just say what I found was at once exhaustive, surprising, and novel.

So, did he still wear me out? Maybe a little. In his defense, for me, thinking big means seeing the forest and glossing over the trees. Brad is the rare "subject matter expert" I've met who manages to see both clearly at once—rare in any discipline, much less in the notoriously shady financial services racket.

It can be a lot to deal with. But I promise you it's worth it. Of course, I'm just a guy in a book. You don't have to take my word for any of this. So why not just turn the page and see for yourself?

—Paul Elliott

1. Thinking Big About Retirement

A bird sitting on a tree is never afraid of the branch breaking, because its trust is not on the branch but on its own wings.

— Charlie Wardle

L et's be the bird.

If that strikes you as a funny way to start a conversation— much less a conversation about planning your retirement— believe me, I hear you. But bear with me. It will all make sense by the time you finish reading this short book.

Along the way, I'll share something I stumbled across at a gathering of moderately subversive *financial planners*, of all things. I don't exaggerate when I say it rocked my world, literally changed the way I think about retirement planning, and would one day spawn the unusual wealth management firm I can tell you about later if you're interested.

And just so you know...

By the time I attended that conference in early 2014, I was no rube. I'd studied economics at Harvard where I took a bachelor's degree with high honors. I'd earned my MBA at Stanford, working under Nobel Laureate Bill Sharpe, who we'll talk more about just ahead.

I'd spent a decade as a management consultant, launched and ran my own business, and hand-built the marketing engine for a hundred-million-dollar financial media company (*The Economist* called us "an ethical oasis in an area that is fast becoming a home to charlatans."[1]).

You'll hear more about that, too. If this strikes you as a lot to cram into such a young man's professional life, you're not wrong. But be ready. I'm about to explain everything, including what propelled me into my final, far-and-away most-rewarding professional mission to date: helping aspiring retirees like you reach your goals.

I mention all this now, albeit in passing, mostly to brag and to get your attention. But also so you'll give some serious weight to those simple words that nearly blew me away when I show them to you just ahead. They're among my list of "investment games," which you'll read about in Chapters Seven and Eight.

Even more than that, I hope you'll consider the simple, yet powerful concept we'll explore in depth in Chapter Two and will revisit throughout our discussion. It grew from a little something I picked up, I hesitate to admit, during a boozy bull session with a couple of real con men during my days peddling stock tips.

(Now, *there's* a chapter of my life I look back on with some trepidation, as we'll also discuss in detail.) At the time, it seemed like so much bourbon-fueled "coffee is for closers" sales guy chest thumping. But the more I thought about it over the years, the more I realized those jokers were on to something.

And that something was this...

If you really want to *sell* someone something, they insisted, you have to sell them on the DEEP BENEFIT. (And if we're being honest, isn't that kind of what's going on here, right now? Only instead of trying to sell you *something*, I want to sell you an *idea*, though it's admittedly a big one.)

So what exactly is the DEEP BENEFIT? If you've ever worked in sales or marketing, you already have some idea. If you haven't dabbled in sales (or, dare I say, evangelism), maybe you can guess. Either way, an example might get us on the same page...

---

[1] Mann, B. (2016).

Imagine we're scoping out the neighborhood martial arts or yoga studio. Now ask yourself this: What is it we're really after? On one level, we're looking to learn some flashy new techniques. Techniques are cool. They're what drive exhibitions that attract new students to the discipline, after all.

On a slightly deeper level, we'll be learning how to fight or keep our balance or bolster our strength or discover our center. Which, let's face it, is also cool. But if you think about it, we're seeking something bigger—something deeper. And it has nothing to do with fighting, or stretching, or sitting, or breathing, or any other "technique."

So, what is it? In my experience, it's the irrevocable permission to go anywhere, at any time, with anybody, in utter ease and with the unshakable assurance you are fully centered and prepared to handle yourself—and handle anything or anybody that might come your way!

Well, that's exactly how I want you to approach this book. You'll pick up some valuable techniques, sure—some might seem like common sense, some might strike you as a little more adventurous and involved, still others will be downright sophisticated, in some cases novel—even proprietary.

More important, you'll walk away with a better, deeper understanding of investments, financial markets, the implications of taxes—even life and financial goal setting, how to think about money, and tactical financial and retirement planning. All of which you can use, beginning right now.

You might even have some fun.

My sincere wish, however, is that you go home with all these things and more, PLUS something much, much bigger. So, what is it? It's what I call *relaxed confidence.* That's right, just as in your neighborhood dojo or yoga shala, relaxed confidence is the very essence of everything I want to share with you today, beginning in the next chapter.

If that sounds a little "out there," don't worry. It sounds whacky to me too. So how about we plunge ahead and I'll show you what I mean?

But First Things First...

My name is Bradley Clark, and I like thinking big.

When I talk about thinking big, I don't mean thinking boldly—I'm no Elon Musk or Jeff Bezos. I have no illusions. To me, thinking big means thinking broadly, holistically, and strategically.

Thinking big means taking a big problem (like how to fund your retirement or achieve a sense of relaxed confidence about money) breaking it down into lots of little pieces, considering each piece from multiple perspectives, then reassembling those pieces into a simple, compelling picture.

Thinking big means smashing silos everywhere you see them (we all operate in silos, after all). It's not even our fault. When every profession or discipline spawns its own ideas and jargon and constructs, it's only natural to get stuck in a single, predictable way of thinking.

Thinking big is a way to get out of an intellectual rut.

Thinking big will help you develop a deeper understanding of your life, your goals, your relationship with money, and, yes, your retirement finances. Thinking big will help you find your confidence. Thinking big will help you relax.

More than anything, thinking big will help you solve problems, beginning with this once-seemingly impenetrable conundrum I've been chewing on for decades:

"How do I support my ideal lifestyle through my retirement, while truly enjoying a feeling of relaxed confidence for the rest of my life?"

Easy to ask. Harder to answer. Harder still to actually achieve!

Yet, even as a very young man, when my whole life was ahead of me, I was obsessed with this challenge, struggling to understand how *just one single pile of money* can generate income and even wealth for the rest of someone's life. Maybe you've wondered the same thing.

If so, you might have realized that the **accumulation phase** of life, when you are building your retirement nest egg, is actually the easy part: work hard, live below your means, max out your 401(k), and select diversified, low-cost investments. There's not much else required for building wealth!

But as you approach and enter the **decumulation phase**, that period of life usually called retirement, when you are hatching your accumulated nest egg and actually *living off that money*—suddenly there are more twists and turns, more risks and more decisions to make.

A big one, obviously, is the very real concern you won't be able to maintain your lifestyle over the long term, no matter how much you've accumulated. Even as you struggle to figure out just how big that pile of money should be and how to make it last, and it's an immense source of worry.

Of course, that's not the only (what I call) *component risk* we face when approaching and ultimately entering retirement that, once you've put your life of paid work behind you, can threaten your financial security, like...

- Stock market performance
- Inflation
- Interest rates
- Long-term care expenses
- Tax policy

Those are just a few of the external factors that affect whether, when, and how comfortably you'll be able to retire. To say nothing of your own longevity and medical needs, which are largely unforeseeable.

I won't sugarcoat it: Figuring out how to address and overcome those challenges, and countless others we'll discuss in this book, is a major task! Especially when you consider that as the big day creeps nearer, and your time available to overcome setbacks diminishes, the stakes get higher and higher.

In my experience, there are two primary approaches to attacking this sticky problem. Both methods have benefits and drawbacks— but don't worry. There is hope, and a possible third way out. I'll do my best to give them both to you by the end of this book.

Solution #1—Carve Your Own Path

When it comes to managing your wealth and planning your dream retirement, it's entirely possible to make your way on your own.

However, be warned. You'll need several things to be able to pull this off yourself. Among others we'll discuss at length in this book, you'll most certainly need...

- *Time* to conduct the research, develop a plan, put it in place, monitor your plan, and adjust your strategies as needed.

- *Mastery* of a wide variety of financial concepts and disciplines, or exceptional research and synthesis skills to ensure you're making the right decisions.

- *Willingness* to be hands-on with your finances, essentially "on call" twenty-four-seven, for *the rest of your life*.

To say nothing of an awareness of your own cognitive biases and how they affect your decision-making, control over your impulses and behavior (even in the face of gut-wrenching market gyrations), and some pretty high-level planning skills.

Most important, you'll need to stay away from the toxic waste dumped into the market by manufacturers of investment and insurance products—and manage to learn on your own how to think catastrophically and plan accordingly.

Again, a decent number of smart folks can pull this off in the beginning and middle of their accumulation phase. It's easier to cut through the weeds when you have income options and the time to recover from any serious tangles.

As you get closer to the decumulation phase, however, the challenges and complexities of planning your retirement increase rapidly. The retirement planning landscape begins to look a lot more forbidding.

Potential Solution #2—Have the Path Cleared for You

The second option you may have considered is working with a professional financial advisor—someone who can cut through the complexity and keep you from getting too deep into the weeds. While this strategy can work, it brings its own complement of risks and problems.

For one thing, financial advisors toil under troubling conflicts of interest, most of which emerge from their compensation structures. Thus, even while most are well-intentioned, even the most professional financial advisors can lose sight of their own conflicts when their compensation is on the line. We'll talk about these conflicts and how they can wreck your retirement in Chapter Thirteen.

Second, most financial advisors lack a specialty in retirement income planning, whether because they're focused on selling specific, narrow solutions (like life insurance or annuities), fixated on out-performing investments, or because their approach is simply too broad to allow for expertise in any one area.

Finally, and perhaps most important, let's say you find a wealth manager with the skills, expertise, and ethics to tackle this problem. If that wealth manager is charging you the industry standard fee of 1% of your assets (or $30,000 *per year* to manage a $3 million portfolio), they are dramatically undermining the exact spending, saving, and investment goals they're supposedly trying to help you achieve!

So, are you ready to fly?

I hope I'm not making this sound too simple (or too foreboding). Or giving you the impression I don't understand what a jungle it can be out there and how easily you can get overwhelmed when even the most basic questions can seem downright troublesome to answer.

Again, I hear you! After all, even before you jot down your most basic financial goal or most rudimentary long-term "plan" you've got ask yourself and answer some serious questions. For example …

- *When* do you want to retire?
- When can you *afford* to retire?
- How do you want to *live* when you retire?

To say nothing of addressing more tactical, down in the weeds considerations like:

- How much do you need to retire?
- Which financial strategies are the soundest?
- Where can you turn for real, useful help?

Unfortunately, there are so many complex strategies available for making the most of your money it can seem impossible to decide. You might wind up feeling lost, frustrated, and no closer to answers than you were when you first started looking!

Of course, some of this might sound familiar.

It's not uncommon to feel we've been blown off course—or to get stuck focusing on the minute details of everyday life. Whether it's our work, our personal life, or our long-term financial plans, we all get lost in the weeds and suffer the confusion and frustration that results.

It's not all bad. Our ability to focus on complex, minute details is part of what makes many of us successful, after all; attention to detail and making sense of complex information are important skills. However, it's just as crucial to see the forest for the trees and navigate your way through it.

Especially when it comes to money. It's easy to get sucked into the chatter of financial experts and analysts predicting the next market crash, or the incessant buzz about this week's hot stock. Even as the background hum of our own financial worries and anxieties drowns out any hope for peace, quiet, and contentment.

It's a lot to deal with. Now, here's some good news. Since you picked up this book, you already suspect there must be another, easier way of doing things—a way to fly through the forest of retirement planning with a sense of confidence and ease. You sense there's a clear path out of the tangle and into the fresh air—and you're right!

Let's be the bird!

If I promise you one thing today, it's that I will always be straight with you. What we're about to discuss can be flat-out intimidating. You'll be moving from the secure world of "work" to a period of your life where you have no alternative but to live on the money you've accumulated. Frankly, it's a high-stakes undertaking.

It's absolutely critical that you're ready to take flight before you leap off the branch. But believe me when I say it: you can do this! So before we get started, here's a short checklist to make sure you're in just the right place at just the right time.

By all means I implore you to read on, if you…

- Recently retired or will do so within the next five years. (If you plan to retire more than five years from now, you might still want to keep reading. There's a lot here for everyone. Just know that some of the strategies in this book won't be relevant for you yet.)

- Have $2 million or more in investable assets. (Again, if you have a little less than that, don't worry. Many of the ideas I'll share with you will still be useful; in fact, much of what you'll read today is "aspirational.")

- Currently work with a professional financial advisor, wealth manager, or retirement planner and want to be a more informed client or are thinking about switching advisors.

Are you still with me? Great. Because, as usual, that's just for starters. You'll also want to keep reading if you...

- Manage your own money and financial affairs and are looking for more, or more sophisticated, ideas and hands-on tactics you can use as you approach your own retirement planning.

- Want to know the best ways to navigate the myriad financial risks you're facing now and will most certainly face in retirement—or in the days and years leading up to the day you put your working life behind you.

- Feel anxiety about your current investments, long-term finances, or retirement plans and want access to more tools and strategies to alleviate that anxiety.

If you simply wonder what's going on inside your brain when you think (or worry) about money in general or your finances in retirement in particular, this book is for you.

If *any* of that sounds familiar, then this book is for you.

So buckle up. In the coming pages, we'll touch on a wide range of concepts from a variety of fields and disciplines including, but not limited to: personal finance, investing, risk management, behavioral economics, psychology, work-life balance, and much more.

Many of these concepts you'll have already encountered. But I'm willing to bet you've never seen them like this. I guess you might say you've seen the trees in this forest before; but as you read this book, you'll truly take flight and see them all from a whole new vantage point. If I'm wrong, by all means write me and let me know!

So, are you ready to be the bird?

2. Confidence & Retirement

Achieving a sense of confidence in retirement requires a great financial plan—and we'll go through exactly what that planning habit looks like later—but it isn't just about the money. While it might seem strange to begin a book on financial planning with a discussion of confidence, confidence is an essential component of everything to come.

A robust financial planning habit is important for building confidence, but confidence in your finances is far from the whole picture.

There is, in fact, a steep *psychological* cost to retirement that can far outweigh any confidence you have in your finances alone. Retiring can produce a surprising range of negative feelings for those who aren't prepared for the impact of the shift from work to retirement life. Too few of us pause to think about that cost until we're already retired and starting to pay it.

I'll explain what I mean with a story from my own life.

Until 2007, my life was characterized by an uninterrupted string of educational and professional accomplishments. I graduated from Harvard and Stanford. I was promoted quickly and multiple times within an elite consulting firm. I co-founded and then sold Military.com before becoming the publisher and Chief Marketing Officer at The Motley Fool, a private financial investing and advice company, where I went on to lead a huge growth surge and business transformation.

I had spent my entire life living in Washington, D.C., San Francisco, and Cambridge. I was accustomed to big cities, fast-paced and aggressive work settings, and regular accolades for my professional achievements.

Then, in 2007, my wife and I decided to leave D.C. and resettle in a small town in New Hampshire.

I'd been feeling a sense of conflict over my work with The Motley Fool, so resigning wasn't as much of a hardship as I expected—at least, not right away. Between 2003 and 2007, I had quadrupled The Motley Fool's revenue by shifting to subscriptions over advertising. I enjoyed the status, influence, compensation, and recognition that went with the position.

But at the same time, something hadn't felt quite right. Despite my belief that it's more prudent for individual investors to put their money in low-cost index funds, I was responsible for helping persuade millions of people to pay for our stock picks.

This nagging conflict of interest helped convince me to make the move to New Hampshire, and to leave my role at The Motley Fool even though I didn't have another job lined up.

Without knowing it, I was about to embark on what was essentially early retirement. I had no idea what a toll it would take.

When we got to New Hampshire, I had no job and no plan. I also discovered that New England can be quite parochial and isn't terribly welcoming to outsiders. Not only did I not have a job, but I also had no local friends.

Slowly, I came to recognize that I had given up my status, influence, compensation, and recognition. Although it wasn't obvious to me at the time, my confidence was already taking a hit.

I decided to start my own company, managing an advertising program for The Motley Fool. While I thought that staying connected to the company would return some of my lost status and influence, I found that being a vendor was a completely different experience: I was no longer in the thick of the action. I no longer had the influence and recognition I was used to.

I also made the mistake of working out of my basement, which increased my feelings of isolation. The work wasn't challenging or rewarding and, without my realizing it, my confidence was quickly draining away.

At the end of 2010, I struck up a conversation with a guy I met on a train, and he offered me a job. Despite the low pay, it seemed like a good opportunity to regain some status, influence, and responsibility.

I was wrong.

Just 18 months after I started, I was fired. My working style—fast-paced, assertive, and a little edgy—simply wasn't a good fit for the organization.

I'd never been fired before. I felt completely humiliated. I wondered how I would ever be able to find, much less thrive in, another job. I spent the next three years under-employed, struggling to regain the sense of confidence and drive that had shaped my career and my life prior to that point.

During that time, I felt like I'd lost my prized ability to think clearly. I struggled to make decisions, form new professional relationships, or understand what my purpose was. I felt like a failure.

All these feelings are surprisingly common among retirees.

Losing a position of power and prestige, giving up your income, and feeling isolated from the people and activities that were once the center of your day can be a devastating experience if you're not prepared for it.

Fortunately, it's possible to overcome it!

Things shifted for me in 2015, when several factors came together to help me rebuild my confidence.

First, I read a couple of books that shook me to my foundations—I'll talk about them in more detail through the rest of this book.

The first was *Mindset*, by Carol Dweck. Dweck's work helped me understand that my confidence had been shattered in part because I had such a strong fixed mindset. I was unable to see my struggles and failures as learning experiences; instead, they felt to me like an indictment of my own worth as a person.

The second book was Daniel Kahneman's *Thinking, Fast and Slow*, and his writing about the power of optimism. I was particularly moved by his observation that if you could have one wish for your unborn child, it should be to wish they'd be born an optimist. I had always prided myself on being a realist, but cultivating optimism changed everything.

Through reading those books and other works on psychology, I came to realize that I was a realist with a fixed mindset and not much resilience. That's not a great set of conditions for maintaining confidence in the face of adversity! And we all face adversity sooner or later.

So, I set about changing my mindset, building resilience, and learning how to think differently. I focused on identifying small, achievable next steps rather than big, vague goals. I challenged my negative thoughts. I started making connections again. I stopped judging and analyzing myself—I gave myself a break.

And through that process, I found meaning. I was finally able to see what I was meant to do: form my own financial advisory practice and help clients.

I had always felt strongly about financial advising, and when I made the decision to open my own firm, it felt as though I was walking on air. Even before my first client walked through the door, I felt confident again. I knew I had the skills, the belief, and the determination to help people.

My journey back into confidence instilled a belief in me that my goal was to help my clients with more than just the financial details— that what I was selling wasn't just financial planning and investment management.

My firm's mission statement reflects that belief: "To help our clients achieve the feeling of relaxed confidence in their financial lives."

Now, I think about achievement differently. I still value achievement, but I've reframed its meaning in my life. I am in service to my clients, helping them achieve the feeling of relaxed confidence. The benefit is that I have never been more relaxed or more confident than I am now, and people respond to relaxed confidence in a big way.

Let me show you how this often plays out. A couple came into my office in mid-2021. Tom and Alyssa were in their mid-50s and had a vague sense that they'd probably be able to retire anywhere from three to eight years in the future. They had a $2.5 million portfolio, Tom's pension, and a ton of questions.

After I crunched the numbers, I told Tom and Alyssa that they wouldn't have to wait eight years to retire. They wouldn't even have to wait three years. With their portfolio and spending goals, they could retire in *two years*.

Initially, Tom was skeptical and more than a little nervous. Would their money last if he retired that soon?

I walked Tom through a fair amount of quantification and numerous scenarios in our planning software to show him and Alyssa how different retirement dates would enable different levels of spending—while also providing them with a robust income floor (a concept we'll talk about in Chapter Six) that would last for the rest of their lives.

Over time, Tom got more comfortable with the idea of retiring sooner than he'd expected. His newfound visibility into his financial situation allowed him to see the stability he'd have regardless of what the stock market might do. Soon after those conversations, Tom set a target retirement date. He'll retire early and get to enjoy that early retirement with Alyssa. If he works, it's because he chooses to.

I love having those conversations, and I get to have them pretty often! While some clients choose to continue working, a lightbulb goes off for others—and many of them start making concrete retirement plans soon after we meet.

There's nothing I like more than being the bearer of good news and showing my clients exactly how to choose a financial plan for retirement that leaves them feeling their own sense of relaxed confidence!

This experience is one of the reasons I now approach wealth management and financial advising from a new perspective: The goal of retirement is not simply to be wealthy; it's to be wealthy *and able to enjoy it*.

The feeling of relaxed confidence is different from simply knowing you've achieved a specific goal, like funding your retirement savings, and it's different from confidence alone.

Relaxed confidence is a sense of confidence that is free from worry, anxiety, or tension. We'll explore both confidence and relaxed confidence in this chapter. The psychological cost of retirement can be steep—but you can work on cultivating a sense of relaxed confidence that helps buffer you against it.

The Psychological Costs of Retirement

Your retirement years can come with a hefty emotional price tag. Rather than the feelings of freedom and relaxation we tend to expect upon retirement, the post-work years can instead become a period of deep unhappiness.

There are several reasons for this, and they help explain why cultivating a sense of relaxed confidence is a critical part of any retirement plan.

Your Confidence Decays

The first reason that focusing on relaxed confidence is so important is that it turns out we *lose* confidence when we retire, and when we age during retirement. It's more important to find ways to feel a sense of relaxed confidence when you retire than before!

A study published by the Journal of Personality and Social Psychology found that confidence tends to peak at age 60, right around the time that many of us are starting to think about retiring.[2] After that, confidence begins to decline.

The decline in self-esteem in our older and post-retirement years tends to be explained by what the study calls "unfavorable changes in income and employment status."[3] That is, we lose our paycheck and any positions of importance, power, or status that came with our employment.

I gave up my paycheck and a position of influence and prestige

---

[2] Orth., et al (2010).
[3] Ibid.

when I left The Motley Fool and its audience of millions, and the next several years did not include a return to power and status! My confidence decayed quickly.

As a professional approaching retirement, odds are you're at a high point in your career. You may have a position of some prestige in your industry, people probably regard you as a mentor and leader, and you likely feel a sense of comfort and power because of both your work and your income.

Once you retire, all that goes away: You no longer have a career or the prestige that went with your title. You're not leading people anymore. You don't have any work to do—and instead of bringing in income, you're now living off your investments and savings.

If you're anything like I was when I hit my period of "early retirement" and your sense of self is wrapped up in your professional achievements, then the psychological cost of retirement for you could be high indeed. The blow to your confidence after the first blush of retirement wears off might be significant.

Your Mind and Body Change

Declining physical health because of age packs another punch when it comes to our confidence, according to Orth and other researchers.[4]

As we get older, we can no longer tackle the world like we could in our 20s—or even our 40s or 50s. Cognitive decline and chronic health problems also appear as we age, further affecting self-esteem.

It's hard to feel confident when it seems like you can no longer rely on your own body.

Avoiding the Cost

A loss of confidence is connected to negative outcomes like anxiety and depression—the antithesis of the relaxed confidence that is your goal for your retirement years. Even if you feel supremely

---

[4] Ibid.

confident in your finances, career, and life right now—which you likely do if you're close to that confidence peak at age 60—it's important to be aware of how your confidence levels might change once you enter retirement.

Fortunately, you don't just have to pay the psychological cost. Instead, you can start to develop a better understanding of what relaxed confidence is and learn how to create it for yourself, no matter what stage of life you're in.

Your Ultimate Goal—The Greatest Gift

I used to think confidence in financial planning meant helping my clients set a course to achieve financial goals like, "I want to maintain my current lifestyle for the rest of my life," or "I want to spend my retirement years traveling."

As I worked on rebuilding my own confidence and cultivating a sense of relaxed confidence, I started to think more deeply about the importance of confidence as a component of my clients' wealth management.

Most financial advisors are content with getting a good financial plan in place and leaving it at that. I've realized that achieving a feeling of relaxed confidence in our financial lives is really the goal; the financial plan itself is just one component.

Relaxed confidence is a mental state that helps make retirement a positive, enjoyable experience, rather than a time of declining confidence and reduced well-being.

You can have the best financial plan on earth, but if your confidence is shattered when you enter retirement, it won't matter. All the exciting spending goals in the world will turn to ash if you lack confidence and spend your time feeling anxious.

This is a book about retirement planning—but more than that, it's a book about how to approach retirement with a sense of relaxed confidence. As we move through the different chapters of this book, I'll explain what relaxed confidence looks and feels like, what its benefits are, and how to achieve it.

What is Confidence?

Many of us intuitively sense that confidence is a good thing, but it can be hard to put our finger on exactly what it is. What defines confidence? What does it feel like? Where does it come from? The word confidence comes from a Latin word that literally means "trusting in oneself," which is a pretty good summary!

Confidence is belief in yourself, and can also encompass belief, trust, or certainty about an approach, another person, or a system.

Confidence is a quiet inner knowledge about your own capabilities. It's the inner peace that comes from feeling like you are prepared and knowing that you can handle whatever happens.

Confidence also comes from understanding your capabilities and developing resilience in the face of failure. As MLB pitcher R. A. Dickey wrote, the best pitchers have a "short-term memory and a bulletproof confidence."[5] The best performance and the strongest confidence comes from focusing not on defeats, but on knowing that you can achieve what you set your mind to.

What's important to understand here is that confidence should be derived from *internal qualities*, not *external achievements*. That is, you don't need to pin your confidence on your ability to manage a team, earn a lot of money, or run a successful business—those are all external metrics of confidence that will disappear in retirement.

Instead, you can learn to reframe confidence in terms of your ability to connect with and lead other people in any circumstance, create conditions for an enjoyable, comfortable life, and approach difficult challenges with trust in your own ability to solve them. Those are all internal metrics of confidence that will be with you for your entire life.

So that's confidence. We can probably all agree that confidence is a good thing to develop!

---

[5] Dickey, R. A. and Coffey, W. (2012).

Beware False Idols

I want to offer a word of caution about confidence. When I talk about confidence, I'm pushing you to develop *true* confidence—confidence that is justifiable and evidence-based.

You will never be able to feel a sense of relaxed confidence if you suffer from overconfidence or hubris, arrogance, or false confidence. Here's why.

Overconfidence or hubris is a type of excessive confidence, a cognitive bias that tells you you're better at things than you really are.

If you are overconfident, you're likely to overestimate your ability to perform something successfully or feel like you have greater knowledge than those around you. This type of biased confidence can result in poor judgment calls in areas where your overconfidence comes into play and tends to be off-putting rather than energizing to other people.

Arrogance is an exaggerated sense of your own importance.

Entering your retirement years will quickly puncture any type of inflated ego you bring with you, as you watch your former prestige and power disappear seemingly overnight. Unlike relaxed confidence, arrogance does not inspire engagement in other people, but instead makes them feel small and resentful.

False confidence happens when you pretend to feel more confident than you are.

While you might convince those around you that you're confident, you'll never be able to achieve a state of relaxation. You'll always be waiting for someone to discover that you aren't as good as you said you were, and that type of stress will erode your stores of resilience and your ability to find peace.

True confidence comes from within. It emerges from a genuine, realistic understanding of your own skills and competence, your willingness to trust in yourself and the systems you have created to support your life, and the knowledge that you can handle any bumps in the road.

True confidence, rather than overconfidence or false confidence, is humble. It will fill you with a sense of satisfaction and draw other people to you, rather than pushing them away.

What is Relaxed Confidence?

You've learned about confidence—and about the types of false confidence to watch out for—but what about *relaxed* confidence?

Having confidence does not necessarily mean you're relaxed. I'm a pretty confident person these days, but I'm still working on the relaxation side of things!

Relaxation means you are free from tension and anxiety, that you are at ease in your surroundings. Personal productivity expert David Allen refers to true relaxation as having a "mind like water."[6] The concept is borrowed from world-class martial artists and is a "mental and emotional state in which your head is clear, able to create and respond freely, unencumbered with distractions and split focus."[7]

Relaxed confidence is belief in yourself coupled with a calm mental and emotional state that is free from undue worry.

The best thing about relaxed confidence is that it is a state that you can achieve in your retirement finances—and that will spill over into the rest of your life as well.

When you know that your financial stability is assured, you can face problems head-on without worrying that they will affect your ability to make ends meet.

When you know that your retirement financial plan is sound, you can greet new opportunities with a sense of excitement, rather than worrying about all the ways things could go wrong.

When you achieve a state of relaxed confidence in your finances, you will feel the benefits across the board.

---

[6] Allen, D. (2002).
[7] Allen, D. (2012).

6 Ways Relaxed Confidence Will Help You

Cultivating a sense of relaxed confidence provides six key benefits, especially in retirement.

Comfort

Relaxed confidence will help you be more comfortable making decisions and focusing on the future.

Instead of finding yourself paralyzed by indecision or constantly worrying about bad things that might happen, you will be able to approach decision-making comfortably, plan for the worst, and return your focus to enjoying the present.

Happiness

Relaxed confidence produces a happier, more positive attitude towards life.

Whereas a loss of confidence in retirement can produce depression, cultivating a sense of relaxed confidence will allow you to appreciate the benefits of retirement and look forward to the rest of your life.

Reduced Worry

Relaxed confidence reduces negative thoughts and worry.

The loss of confidence many people experience in retirement produces anxiety about the future and rumination about what could happen. Developing an attitude of relaxed confidence allows you to acknowledge the possibility of bad outcomes while also knowing you've planned for them and can handle whatever comes your way.

Resilience

Relaxed confidence contributes to your stores of resilience, which you'll need to draw on if something negative does occur—and it inevitably will.

If you spend all your time fretting and feeling stress, then your stores of energy for dealing with a negative event will always be low. When something does happen, you'll have a harder time handling it. Creating the conditions for relaxed confidence means that if a difficult situation arises, you'll be well-equipped to respond productively.

Inner Peace

Relaxed confidence is closely associated with a stronger sense of inner peace.

Think about it: if you approach life with a relaxed attitude and a sense of internal confidence, you're much more likely to also feel peaceful.

Health

Relaxed confidence also contributes to a healthier life!

Spending your time in a state of worry or stress leads to negative health outcomes. As we'll discuss in Chapter Three, relaxed confidence and optimism are two incredible tools for improving your health outcomes over the long term. It's especially important to develop relaxed confidence in retirement when health concerns can become more significant.

But It's Not Just About You!

A feeling of relaxed confidence offers a range of individual benefits—and you're not the only one who will be positively affected by it. Your relaxed confidence can also help the people you love.

As the great football coach Vince Lombardi put it, "Confidence is contagious...so is lack of confidence." If you feel uncertain and anxious, you'll wind up passing that attitude to the people around you. A lack of confidence can create a negative emotional spiral that brings everyone down.

However, someone who gives off a genuine sense of relaxed confidence is magnetic. Not only do they feel good themselves, but they also make other people feel good too. We all know someone who has a simply infectious positive energy. Everyone enjoys being around that type of person because they also lead us to feel more engaged and motivated.

I've seen this play out in my own work with clients. During one meeting with my clients Jerry and Jeanette, the question of Jeanette's retirement came up. Jerry is 69 and retired, while Jeanette is 67 and still working. Jeanette told me she felt she needed to keep her job for financial security, and she and Jerry worried about their spending.

This is not an uncommon problem: many people who accumulate assets over their working years struggle to spend that money in retirement. Relying on your assets rather than your income can be a challenging mental shift!

I worked with Jeanette to run a few simulations that showed the financial impact her retirement would have if she kept working for five years, three years, or if she retired immediately.

The simulations showed that there would be no negative financial impact if Jeanette quit her job that very day—and that, in fact, she and Jerry could increase their annual spending without any negative impact!

As Jeanette's understanding of their financial situation improved, her sense of relaxed confidence increased as well. She decided to continue working, but only because knowing she didn't need the job made her enjoy it more.

Jeanette's newfound feelings of relaxed confidence also affected Jerry's feelings about their finances. Jerry got comfortable with a higher level of spending, a breakthrough after his years of analysis and worry.

As you develop a sense of relaxed confidence with regard to your own retirement finances, you'll be able to see its positive impact on everyone you interact with.

Conclusions

Retirement can exact a high psychological cost if you're not prepared for it, but there are ways to cultivate a sense of relaxed confidence in retirement—and your financial plan is only one component of it. Developing a sense of relaxed confidence is tied to your ability to implement your retirement financial plan.

There are several major ways to cultivate a sense of relaxed confidence in your own life—including your finances—which we'll explore throughout the rest of this book. Some of the components of relaxed confidence include optimism, goal-setting, and resilience, which we will discuss in the upcoming chapters.

Key Takeaways

- Confidence tends to peak at age 60 and then decay—and retirement plays a role in this, due to lost prestige, power, and income.

- Cognitive and physical decline also contribute to lost confidence.

- Confidence and well-being can be maintained in retirement! Confidence is an essential element of a successful retirement plan.

- **Confidence:** Trust/belief in yourself; belief, trust, or certainty about an approach, another person, or a system.

- There are detrimental forms of confidence:
  - Overconfidence or hubris: The belief that you're better at things than you really are.
  - Arrogance: An exaggerated sense of your own importance.
  - False confidence: Pretending to be more confident than you are.

- The goal is a feeling of **relaxed confidence:** Belief in yourself coupled with a calm mental and emotional state that is free from worry.

- Relaxed confidence can support your relationships and provides numerous other benefits:
  - Comfort
  - Happiness
  - Reduced worry
  - Resilience
  - Inner peace
  - Better health

- It is possible to cultivate a sense of relaxed confidence as part of your retirement financial plan.

3. The Engine of Capitalism

Confidence is a powerful tool for overcoming the psychological costs of retirement, but it's not the only one. Optimism is another.

Optimism is a bias towards a sense of well-being, a feeling of hope and confidence, and an attitude or belief that outcomes will be positive. Being optimistic leads people to see events and attributes as favorable to them, to regard the world as benign, and to expect good things to happen.

When we think of cognitive biases, or distorted ways of thinking, we often treat them as bad things. This makes sense: a lot of cognitive biases lead to illogical decision-making, like hanging on to a bad investment or trying to time the stock market.

It's hard to evade our biases because, by their nature, they're hard to notice. There's a whole group of common cognitive biases that can affect our financial choices, and a lot of effort is devoted to outwitting ourselves and coming up with a logical, reality-based financial plan.

Avoiding or overcoming biased thinking is a significant part of developing a sound retirement financial plan and approaching retirement with a sense of relaxed confidence. However, I want to encourage you to think a little differently about bias, and about optimism in particular.

The truth of the matter is that cognitive biases aren't wholly bad; it's not black and white. Bias is a complex subject, and there are some distortions to thinking that can be incredibly powerful.

Optimism is one of those biases.

While naïve optimism is a major risk for your finances, a

productive, well-directed sense of optimism will support your sense of relaxed confidence. We'll talk about how to tell the difference between the two types of optimism in this chapter.

Developing a sense of relaxed confidence necessitates finding a way to be an optimist in your financial life, and cultivating an overall mindset geared towards optimistic thinking.

While we'll discuss the importance of thinking about realism, risk, and resilience in Chapter Five, the benefits of developing a bias toward optimism far outweigh any drawbacks.

Optimism vs. Realism vs. Pessimism

I was born a realist—someone who can see facts and situations clearly, and deal with them accordingly. I grew up a realist, and I stayed a realist for many years. I felt I could see things as they really were, without emotion or bias affecting my thinking.

I was proud of being a realist for a long time. Realism served me well! I made accurate forecasts at work because I was able to see what was likely to happen and describe it with a clear head. I always budgeted enough time for things like getting to the airport because I had a realistic sense of the delays I might encounter along the way.

I cared far more about analysis, evidence, and logic than any touch-feely optimism or weepy, brooding pessimism.

Optimists stand in stark contrast to realists, who strive to see the world as it is, without positive emotion influencing their feelings. The difference between optimists and pessimists is even starker, as pessimists allow negative expectations to color their beliefs.

In general, many of us are already wary of pessimists. People who see the downside of everything and expect the worst outcome aren't exactly the life of the party. However, for much of my life, I was also judgmental of optimists. Optimists struck me as naïve and unrealistic.

For example, while I budgeted my time for delays in getting to the airport, I'd encounter optimists who didn't. They seemed foolish, because they weren't thinking about the possibility of delays, traffic jams, or other problems; they simply assumed things were going to work out for the best.

Analysis and logic pointed to the power of realism in my life, while optimists always seemed to have their heads in the clouds, missing flights and showing up late to important meetings—or having everything somehow work out perfectly. I didn't understand optimism, and I didn't appreciate it.

Then I lost my confidence. As I worked on regaining my confidence, I started reading actual scientific research about pessimism, realism, and optimism, and I learned something shocking. I'd been wrong about optimism—and myself—all along.

Now, I wish I had been born an optimist. Let me tell you why.

The King of All Distortions

Psychologists have spent the past several decades cataloging numerous cognitive biases, helping to explain how and why our brains play tricks on us. Financial analysts have also systematically explained how cognitive biases mean we're pretty much destined to make mistakes when it comes to investing.

Optimism is one of the most significant cognitive biases of them all. So how, you might be wondering, is optimism a good thing?

Although optimism is undoubtedly a cognitive bias, here's why it's the most powerful of the biases, and why I wish I'd been born an optimist: First, optimism contributes to positive self-fulfilling prophecies.

Think of that old Henry Ford quotation: "Whether you think you can, or you think you can't—you're right." Optimism leads us to expect good outcomes, which leads us to work towards good outcomes, which contributes to our chances of achieving good outcomes.

Some of the most significant cognitive biases around finances include things like **loss aversion** (preferring to avoid loss over actions that would produce gains), **hindsight bias** (seeing events from the past as more obvious or predictable than they really were), **self-attribution bias** (taking credit for successes while blaming failures on external factors), and **anchoring bias** (clinging to a reference point, often the first piece of information presented on a topic).

All these biases shape our thinking, and it doesn't take much to see how they prime us to be lousy investors. With just that list in mind, cognitive biases seem like a huge problem for our finances!

NERDING OUT!

When it comes to financial planning, optimism can be an incredibly powerful tool.

Second, there is mounting scientific evidence that optimists are healthier,[8] that they live longer,[9] that they are more successful,[10] and that they have better relationships.[11]

---

[8] Lear, S. (2020).

[9] Lee, L. O., et al. (2019).

[10] Gielan, M. (2019).

[11] Srivastava, S., et al. (2006).

Optimism is a bias, sure, but I don't know too many people who want *worse* health, a *shorter* life, *less* success, or *unsatisfying* relationships!

The 3 Risks of Optimism

Before we dive deeply into the benefits of optimism, I want to acknowledge the risks of optimism for your finances—optimism *is* a cognitive bias, even if my larger argument is that the benefits outweigh those risks.

There are three potential risks associated with optimism and your financial life and knowing what they are is half the battle. Once you've learned the risks of optimism, it becomes much easier to cultivate optimism in a way that is productive for your life and your financial plan.

Failing to Diversify

One of the risks of optimism is failing to diversify your investment portfolio. Let's say you feel extremely optimistic about a new startup—the company seems like they have the next big idea, and you have high expectations. You might even work at the company or be an early investor.

Optimism can tempt you to put way too much money into that one company, simply because you expect good things to happen! After all, it could be the next Amazon!

However, as Nobel Prize-winning psychologist Daniel Kahneman points out in *Thinking, Fast and Slow,* 65% of new businesses fail within five years.[12] Every person in every startup probably feels optimistic about their odds of success, but the math simply goes against them. If optimism leads you to over-invest in a company that goes under, your retirement financial plan could be set back significantly.

---

[12] Kahneman, D. (2011).

I sometimes encounter this type of thinking among my clients. Although my clients tend to be extremely well-educated, intelligent, and successful people, no one is immune to cognitive biases.

Let me give you an example: When Gavin and Kay came to my office, they had a portfolio worth about $50 million. However, close to 97% of that portfolio was tied up in a single stock. To make matters worse, it was the stock of Kay's employer, a startup that had recently gone public and was worth billions.

When confronted with a situation like that, any financial advisor is going to say that the immediate priority is to diversify your holdings. I made that recommendation—but some cognitive biases got in the way.

Optimism was one of those biases. Kay was highly optimistic about her company's prospects. She also suffered from over-confidence about the management team's and her own ability to influence the stock price, and the endowment effect, which leads us to ascribe more value to things that we own than they might have.

Guess what happened: Gavin and Kay elected not to diversify, and the value of the stock dropped to $25 million not long after. Then it popped back up to $35 million, and on and on the rollercoaster went—up one day, down the next. It turned out to be a much more volatile stock than Kay and Gavin originally believed it would.

Eventually, I convinced them to sell $15 million and diversify their portfolio in a way that secured their financial future, no matter how the startup stock continued to gyrate. I quantified exactly what Gavin and Kay needed to sell to meet their needs for the rest of their lives, rather than simply pushing them to sell off a huge chunk of the stock.

Time, quantification, and the continued erratic performance eventually overcame the original cognitive biases that led Kay and Gavin to hang on to such a concentrated position. From the outside looking in, it seems obvious that having nearly all your money tied up in one asset can cost you—and fast—but cognitive biases like optimism create real barriers to good financial decision-making.

We'll talk about some useful strategies for diversifying your portfolio *and* leaving room for optimistic investment explorations in

Chapter Eight. There are ways to play with fire without getting burned!

Although it's important to cultivate optimism about the overall state of the market, it's equally important to diversify your portfolio appropriately. Allow optimism to encourage you to invest—and allow your investing decisions to be guided by sound investment principles.

Failing to Think Catastrophically

While it might seem counter-intuitive to promote catastrophic thinking in a chapter about being optimistic, thinking about risk is important. Taking a Pollyannaish approach to life, or what we might call naïve optimism, can lead us to disregard potential risks, take bigger risks than we can afford, and fail to consider what will happen if the outcome isn't good after all.

Ideally, optimism helps us avoid *ruminating* on catastrophe—it's not that we never consider it at all.

A productively optimistic mindset is one in which you consider catastrophe, make plans for it, and then focus your attention on hoping and planning for the best.

Failing to Find a Good Advisor

Optimists are more likely to seek financial help than pessimists are—but optimism can lead to placing your trust in the wrong type of advisor. There are many financial advisors who lack mastery and objectivity, as we'll discuss in Chapter Thirteen.

If your blanket assumption is that outcomes will be positive, you might simply accept financial advice at face value, trusting that everything will work out okay in the end.

It might! But then again, it might not.

Optimism is best supported by masterful, objective financial advice. In other words, you can outsource your realism (and even your pessimism) to a professional, but it must be a professional who will ensure you have a financial plan that works for your life.

When it's well-directed, optimism can improve nearly every aspect of your life in retirement, including your finances. If you personally still lean more towards the realist side of things, there is even a way for you to harness the optimism of others to improve your odds of financial success!

Betting on Humanity

Kahneman calls optimism the engine of capitalism. As he puts it, "Optimistic individuals play a disproportionate role in shaping our lives,"[13] because optimists are more likely to be entrepreneurs, inventors, and leaders who are willing to take risks—even when those risks don't make sense to a realist (much less a pessimist).

Kahneman notes that only 35% of small businesses survive for five years in the U.S.[14] Put another way, that's a dismal 65% failure rate. Yet most entrepreneurs, when asked, will say their own odds of success are seven out of 10—and a full third say there is a 0% chance they'll fail!

Entrepreneurs, as a group, are suffering from a serious cognitive bias: optimism.

And yet it is this same bias for optimism that fuels the economy by ensuring that entrepreneurs pursue their business ideas, that inventors try to get new inventions to market, and that all of them stay the course in the face of setbacks.

Kahneman points out that, "When action is needed, optimism, even of the mildly delusional variety, may be a good thing."[15] Optimists, even the mildly delusional ones, are the people who get things done.

Marrying optimism with sound financial planning is one way to

---

[13] Ibid.
[14] Ibid.
[15] Ibid.

get things done while still ensuring you live the life you want. Take some of my clients, for example: Cole and Lucy, a married couple in their 40s and 50s with one child in college and another under 10. They wanted to start their own business, but also needed to make sure they could still save for their younger child's education.

The couple was incredibly optimistic about the success of their business venture, but also worried about the financial stress of potential failure.

We modeled three different scenarios for their new business, built a spending framework around each model, and then built out a five-year bond ladder that enabled my clients to move south, pay their bills, and start their business. I also advised them to superfund a 529 plan for their younger child, a strategy I'll talk about in more detail in Chapter Ten.

That's the power of entrepreneurial optimism combined with financial planning: Cole and Lucy were able to move forward into an uncertain future with excitement and confidence rather than worry.

When it comes to optimism and the stock market, it's easy to get sucked into data and analysis. We can slice and dice stock market returns all day, look at the information by time, asset class, and geography, and analyze volatility and correlation—you name it. I've spent countless hours doing just that, but I want to set it all aside for a moment to ask a question.

What if we distilled long-term investing in the stock market down to one elegant idea?

Here it is:

When we invest, we are simply placing our trust and our faith in all 7.9 billion people on the planet, and in our collective optimism.

While not everyone is an optimist, enough of us are. In fact, a Life is Good Optimism and Positivity Survey found that a full 85% of Americans describe themselves as optimistic![16]

Optimists are the people who are going to take the "illogical" entrepreneurial risks that will end up driving breathtaking innovation. The people taking those risks will be the ones who create the next Amazon, and the next 30 Amazons after that. And it's quite likely that, if we invest in the stock market, our portfolios will benefit from their optimism over the long term.

We'll cover the risks and benefits of investing in Chapters Seven, Eight, and Nine, but the basic idea is this: We have no way of predicting which investment will pay off, so we should own all the stocks.

What we're doing in that case is harnessing optimism by placing our trust in the engine of capitalism rather than in individual entrepreneurs or companies. No matter how pessimistic you might be individually, you can rely on the optimism of others to help build your wealth.

Betting on a single company is an example of how optimism can backfire. It might work out, but the odds are against you, no matter how optimistic you feel about today's hot stock or shiny new startup.

Instead, opt for the type of optimism that encourages you to have faith in the stock market over the long term, rather than putting all your eggs in one basket. In this way, you can balance a realistic approach to investing with an optimistic mindset about the market across time.

A Virtuous Cycle

Even if you plan to completely outsource your wealth management, optimism is an important component of your retirement financial plan and the development of relaxed confidence.

---

[16] Life is Good (2018).

Let's return to the idea of confidence for a moment. In the last chapter, we defined confidence as trusting in yourself. Confidence can also be trust in another person, in an approach, or in a system—such as trust that the optimism that fuels the market will contribute to your portfolio.

Confidence and optimism are closely related, although the two concepts are slightly different. Confidence is about trust and justified belief; optimism is about positive hope and expectations.

So does optimism drive confidence, or does confidence drive optimism? Personally, I see them as inextricably linked, part of a virtuous cycle.

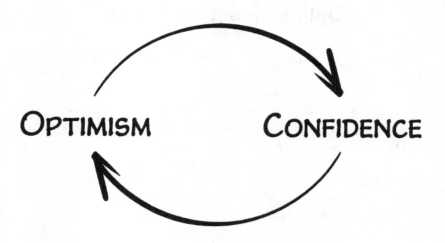

Optimism drives confidence. As professor and career mentor Bud Bilanich says, "Optimism is the foundation on which all self-confidence is built."[17] If you're already primed to believe the outcome will be positive, it's much easier to take risks that will lead to greater confidence—trust in your skills and abilities. Optimism provides the impetus for taking actions that bolster confidence.

---

[17] Bilanich, B. (2008).

Confidence also drives optimism. Psychotherapist Karol Ward says that "When you feel confident, you feel much more optimistic about life."[18] Evidence-based confidence, that internal sense of your own capabilities, supports an attitude of optimism. If you already know you have the skills you need to accomplish a task, it's easier to adopt a more favorable outlook and to feel that the outcome will be positive.

These two attributes are not a chicken-and-egg conundrum, but rather play off one another in powerful ways, and cultivating both confidence and optimism will positively affect your life and your retirement planning. Here's how.

Optimism & Your Money

Financial optimism has several benefits. A 2018 study by Michelle Gielan and Frost Bank[19] demonstrated connections between optimism and positive financial outcomes, including reduced stress, better financial health, and an easier time adjusting to setbacks.

While the study does not indicate whether optimism directly led to these outcomes, there are clear connections between optimism and good finances. The study also indicates some of the ways that pessimism can lead to worse financial outcomes, in part by leading to learned helplessness, or the sense that no action will help in the face of negative circumstances.

It's possible that preexisting positive financial circumstances created feelings of optimism for study participants, which in turn supported better outcomes and decision-making.

It's also possible that optimists were able to achieve better outcomes because of their more positive mindset, which led them to seek solutions, ask for help, and follow through on advice.

The main takeaway of this study should not be that optimism is a cure-all or a guarantee of financial success. What the study *does* show

---

[18] Steinhilber, B. (2017).
[19] Gielan, M. (2018).

us is that optimism helps create habits and promotes behaviors that are strongly associated with better financial—and better overall—outcomes.

Optimists Feel Less Money Stress

It's true! According to the results of the study, optimists are less stressed out about their finances than realists or pessimists.[20] In fact, optimists spend 145 fewer days worrying about money each year than pessimists do.

On average, an optimist worries about money for 81 days a year—while a pessimist spends 226 days worrying about money! That is a significant gap.

Imagine how you want to spend your retirement years. Do you want to spend more than 60% of any given year worrying about your finances? I don't know about you, but I'd rather spend that time focusing on friends, family, travel, and enjoying myself.

Cultivating optimism about your finances will allow you to spend significantly more time focusing on the things you want to enjoy in retirement, rather than worrying about money. Having a strong financial plan is a great way to support an optimistic mindset about your money, and we'll walk through exactly how to set up your retirement finances in the coming chapters.

Optimists Have Better Financial Health

Optimists not only feel less stress about their finances, but their financial well-being is also stronger than that of pessimists. The study found that 62% of optimists show signs of strong financial health—seven times higher than pessimists, who clock in at an unfortunate 9%.[21]

---

[20] Ibid.
[21] Ibid.

Strong financial health includes things like controlling one's finances, avoiding unmanageable debt, having a financial cushion, setting financial goals and being likely to meet those goals, and being able to spend money for enjoyment.

Having poor financial health *and* a pessimistic attitude can lead to a self-perpetuating defeatist cycle.

Picture a pessimist entering retirement without a strong financial buffer who then experiences an expensive health crisis. Their pessimism primes them to expect the worst, making it unlikely that they'll prepare for future financial and medical issues—and when they inevitably experience one, the negative outcomes will reinforce their pessimism.

Optimism, on the other hand, primes individuals to make choices that support their financial health, which make it easier to weather challenges when they do appear. Financial difficulties happen to everyone, but optimists are more likely than pessimists to be prepared for them.

Optimists Are More Likely to Save

One of the reasons that optimists have better financial health is that they're more likely to save money than pessimists. Nearly half of all optimists report that they're good at saving money, compared to only 31% of pessimists.[22]

Further, the same study found that 53% of optimists report making progress on their financial goals, compared to only 38% of pessimists. What that means is that when catastrophe strikes, optimists are going to be better prepared to handle it than pessimists.

The optimists will have spent less time worrying about finances, meaning they have energy left to devote to dealing with the problem. The optimists will also have stores of financial reserves, because they are better at setting and working towards their savings goals. Being an optimist pays off in multiple ways.

---

[22] Ibid.

Optimists Ask for Help

Asking for help can be incredibly challenging, and we'll talk more about that issue in Chapter Thirteen. For now, it's important to note that optimism plays a role!

Optimists are much more willing to get professional financial help than pessimists are—59% of optimists versus 42% of pessimists.[23] Optimism can lead you to expect good outcomes, which means it's much less anxiety-inducing to consider asking for expert advice.

Optimists are also significantly more likely to follow through on the advice they get, according to Gielan's research: More than 60% of optimists that ask for help act on the answers, compared to only 40% of pessimists.

If you think you'll get good results, you're more likely to ask for guidance; if you then follow through on the expert advice you get, you're more likely to see those results come to fruition.

Once again, optimism and confidence will build on each other.

Optimists Adjust to Setbacks

Everyone experiences setbacks in their financial plans and in their lives. It happens! How we respond to those challenges often depends on whether we are approaching difficulties as an opportunity to learn, or an opportunity to complain.

Optimists are much more likely to take setbacks as a chance to learn and change their behaviors. The report found that 69% of optimists put better financial plans in place after hitting a speed bump, while only 36% of pessimists did the same.[24]

Treating setbacks as learning opportunities is another reason optimists are more likely to hit their financial goals.

They still expect good outcomes, even when the path gets a little

---

[23] Ibid.

[24] Ibid.

rocky. All these optimistic habits intertwine with and drive confidence, and vice versa. Optimism is a major part of building a retirement financial plan that contributes to your sense of relaxed confidence.

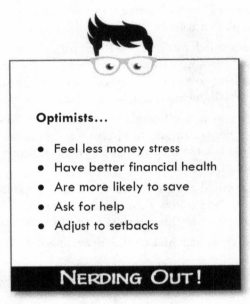

Optimists...

- Feel less money stress
- Have better financial health
- Are more likely to save
- Ask for help
- Adjust to setbacks

NERDING OUT!

A Powerful Antidote

Optimism is also an antidote to another major cognitive bias. **Negativity bias** means that we are psychologically preconditioned to pay attention to threats—our focus is inherently drawn more to the negative than the positive.

Negativity bias was an important trait 30,000 years ago, when a threat meant a large predator was running straight at you. Today, however, our brains still process negative information as threatening—even when it has minimal impact on our immediate physical well-being. Negativity bias thus leads to stress and anxiety, by keeping our focus on perceived "threats" and keeping our minds and bodies constantly alert for danger.

There's a saying in media: If it bleeds, it leads. The saying is another way that negativity bias plays out in our daily lives. We're primed to pay attention to negative news. Negativity bias is also why doomsday predictions and the frantic energy of daytime finance news shows can have such a hold on us.

In the past, I've watched some of my clients consume a lot of financial news media. They often get pulled into focusing on negative predictions, and then they can't let go. They lose the ability to see things any other way, and they become paralyzed by fear.

One man I worked with was a devotee of financial news reports. He had millions of dollars just sitting in a bank account because he was too afraid to invest. Negativity bias prompted him to pay so much attention to doomsday predictions in the financial media that he was always certain the next big market crash was right around the corner.

Instead of putting his money into an investment account that would have increased his wealth and allowed him to fund a relaxed, comfortable life, he clung tightly to his cash. All the while, his spending power eroded, year after year.

Negativity bias and the imagined threat of losing his money prevented him from seeing the negative outcome of *not* investing.

Optimism provides an antidote to the mental and financial poison that is negativity bias and supports your ability to make sound financial choices. If you expect good outcomes, it becomes much easier to let doom and gloom predictions roll off your back—or ignore the financial media entirely and enjoy your life!

Cultivating optimism allows you to see most financial news for what it is: short-term thinking designed to keep you watching, and often inaccurate in its predictions anyway! Optimism helps you acknowledge negativity when you encounter it and then choose where to focus your attention.

Learning and Practicing Optimism

If you were lucky enough to be born an optimist, you probably don't need to work on cultivating an optimistic mindset. For the rest of us, however, there are practical strategies for learning and practicing optimism!

Even if you were born a pessimist, it's surprisingly easy to cultivate optimism and see the positive impact it can have on your life.

Cultivate a Growth Mindset

In her groundbreaking book *Mindset*, Stanford psychologist Carol Dweck described two types of beliefs people have about themselves.[25]

One is a **fixed mindset**, in which someone believes their personality, character, abilities, and intelligence are static—that growth and change are all but impossible.

People with a fixed mindset often fear failure and see success as confirmation of their inherent worthiness and intelligence. A fixed mindset can lead to pessimism and difficulty recovering from setbacks.

Picture, for example, a student with a fixed mindset. When the student does well on tests, they credit their own innate intelligence and abilities for their success and ignore factors like how much they studied.

If that same student fails a test, they're likely to blame that failure on what they see as an innate lack of intelligence or ability. A fixed mindset will not allow the student to consider other factors like not studying enough, not getting enough sleep the night before, or needing more time to understand the material.

A **growth mindset**, on the other hand, is one in which someone believes their personality, character, abilities, and intelligence are fluid—that growth and change are not only possible, but desirable.

People with a growth mindset, like optimists, see failure as a learning opportunity. A growth mindset leads to optimism, an easier

[25] Dweck, C. (2007).

time recovering from setbacks, and often more positive personal and professional relationships.

Picture a different student, this one with a growth mindset. When the student does well on tests, they are able to acknowledge their own skills—*and* they're able to see how all that time studying helped them learn.

If this student fails a test, they're less likely to see themselves as a failure, and will instead take the time to identify opportunities for studying more, getting adequate sleep and nutrition before tests, and asking for help.

A fixed mindset in your financial life can hold you back from making necessary changes that will support your retirement goals. Just for starters, a fixed mindset can keep you feeling like you have nothing left to learn about finances—or feeling like you'll never be able to learn more than you already know.

A fixed mindset leads to focusing on scarcity and giving up in the face of obstacles, because there's no clear path to change. The wonderful thing about research into mindset is that even if you have a fixed mindset now, you can change it!

As Dweck wrote, her research shows that "the view you adopt for yourself profoundly affects the way you live your life."[26] With a fixed mindset, you might be consumed with the constant need to prove yourself and reaffirm your worthiness through external metrics of success.

Cultivating a growth mindset involves training yourself to think about yourself and your life situation in terms of opportunities, instead. Begin to look for opportunities to cultivate the attributes you want and find opportunities to learn—rather than to achieve success or gain accolades.

Adopting a growth mindset is a key strategy for increasing your optimism. If you see yourself as someone capable of growth and change, then you're much more likely to feel hope about the future. The more optimistic you feel, the more likely you are to achieve a sense of relaxed confidence in your finances.

---

[26] Ibid.

Spend Time with Optimists

Like confidence, optimism can be contagious! You've probably heard the saying that you're the average of the five people you spend the most time with, and it's true.

If you spend most of your time around pessimists, you will become more likely to adopt negative attitudes yourself. It's just like consuming all the doom and gloom of financial news: we tend to believe what we surround ourselves with.

If, on the other hand, you develop relationships with optimists, you'll find that your outlook will shift towards a more optimistic one as well. Not only that, but you'll probably have a better time along the way.

People who expect the best, hope for the future, and respond well to setbacks are a lot more fun to be around than pessimists.

Turn Off the News

While it's important to stay informed, information overload and negativity bias will erode your ability to be optimistic.

Staying attuned to the news day in and day out is a surefire way to kill optimism, because the news is going to focus on what's going wrong over what's going right. Find a trustworthy news source to get the information that matters to you, and then turn it off!

Focus your attention elsewhere. You don't have to pretend that things are all sunshine and rainbows, but you *can* decide how you are going to spend your energy.

Choose something hopeful to fill some of your time instead of the news, and you'll be shocked by how much more optimistic you feel.

Notice Your Thoughts

Pay attention to the pessimistic thoughts that arise, as they do for almost all of us now and again. Thoughts like "I knew it wouldn't work," or "I'm never going to recover from this," or "I'm a failure" are all pessimistic thoughts. They keep your attention on the negative and close you off from the possibility of change and happiness.

Cultivate optimism by noticing when those thoughts arrive and find a way to dispute or reframe them.

Instead, challenge yourself to shift your thinking to things like "That didn't work—what can I learn from this?" or "That was rough, but I have the emotional and financial resilience to deal with it. What can I do to move forward again?" or "I'm always learning, and not getting something right the first time is part of the process."

You can become more optimistic by challenging your pessimistic thoughts, and over time, it will be second nature to look at setbacks as opportunities rather than dead ends.

Conclusions

Cultivating a productive, well-directed sense of optimism is a powerful aspect of achieving a sense of relaxed confidence in retirement, since confidence and optimism work hand in hand. In fact, optimism and confidence are the foundation of a successful retirement plan, and a happy, fulfilling life.

In the next several chapters, we're going to explore the other elements required for building your retirement plan, from goal setting and resilience to the specific financial strategies you'll need to put that plan in place.

Key Takeaways

- **Optimism:** A cognitive bias that predisposes someone towards a sense of well-being, feelings of hope and confidence, and an attitude or belief that outcomes will be positive.

- **Cognitive biases:** Thinking distortions that can lead to illogical decision-making.

- Naïve optimism can lead to illogical choices like failing to diversify your portfolio.

- Productive, well-directed optimism is associated with a range of beneficial outcomes, including:
    o Positive self-fulfilling prophecies.
    o Better health.
    o Longer life.
    o Greater success.
    o Better relationships.

- Optimists fuel the economy by taking risks, creating new products/services, and persisting in the face of difficulties.

- When we invest, we are simply placing our trust and our faith in all 7.9 billion people on the planet, and in our collective optimism.

- Optimism is linked to a few other positive financial outcomes, including:
    o Reduced financial stress.
    o Better financial health.
    o Increased savings rates.

o Asking for—and acting on—advice.

o Adjusting to setbacks more easily.

- Optimism is a healthy counter to **negativity bias**, or our propensity to pay more attention to negative news and events.

- You can cultivate optimism even if you are not naturally optimistic!
    - o Develop a **growth mindset**, or a belief that your personality, characteristics, abilities, and intelligence are fluid.
    - o Spend time with optimists.
    - o Turn off the news.
    - o Practice mindfulness and reframing negative thoughts.

- Confidence and optimism build on each other as part of a virtuous cycle that supports a feeling of relaxed confidence in retirement.

4. Getting Your Goals Right

Since you're reading this book, you're probably a lot like me: goal-driven and successful. I have been a goal-driven person all my life—and for a good portion of that time, I was focused on achievement-related goals that would result in external accomplishments.

I did well with this approach for a long time. I received a great education and then went on to a career characterized by significant professional achievements. Money and accolades shaped my life and my goals.

Then my confidence took a tumble. During that time, I learned a lot of lessons about the importance of goals, and of setting the right *kinds* of goals. In fact, my perspective on goals and achievement completely changed!

Now, rather than allowing my financial goals to direct my life, I base all my life goals on my values. Everything flows from my values, and because of that my life goals and financial goals feel more attainable and better aligned with the life I want to live.

VALUES ➡ LIFE GOALS ➡ FINANCIAL GOALS

As I worked on rebuilding my confidence, research on goals and their role in creating a satisfying life helped me shift my approach. I focus on providing help and service to my clients.

Instead of focusing on my own external accomplishments, I've turned my attention to where my values are: helping my clients achieve a sense of relaxed confidence in their finances.

My primary professional goal is assisting my clients in creating the most powerful financial plan possible—one that is in line with their values and their life goals. Whether you work with an advisor or manage your finances on your own, clarifying your values is a critical first step to having a retirement financial plan that fits your life. Getting clear about what your values are is an essential part of setting financial goals that will serve you well.

Confidence and optimism also play a role in identifying the goals that will be right for you. Remember that confidence and optimism exist in a virtuous cycle. You'll want to identify goals you feel both confident and optimistic about reaching—as you reach those goals, your optimism and confidence will increase, allowing you to set new and more ambitious goals.

First Things First: Clarifying Your Values

Knowing and understanding what your values are is essential to designing the life you want to lead in retirement. If you aren't clear on your life and personal values, it becomes easy to get distracted by goals that seem useful or exciting, but that are out of alignment with what you want from your own life.

Values are the principles that shape how we make decisions and find meaning in life.

Everyone's values are unique: one person might list compassion, connection, and dependability as their core values, while another person might prioritize financial security, accomplishment, and success.

Although most of us likely share several values, our core values and how we prioritize them will look different and will shape how we make decisions about retirement and money.

Some finance-specific values associated with building wealth, for example, might include avoiding overspending, increasing income, having a high savings rate, avoiding consumer debt, prioritizing needs over wants, and cultivating gratitude.

Let's look at an example. Through my firm, I worked with a couple who loves to sail—Sharon and Alexander. Their values include adventure, seeing the world, and introducing their teenage son to different cultures—all while staying on track for their larger retirement and financial goals.

They set a goal of sailing around the world with their son before he was an adult, and we were able to build a two-year bond ladder that financed the trip in alignment with their overall values. At the time of this writing, Alexander, Sharon, and their son are sailing across the Pacific Ocean!

As you continue reading this book, take some time to identify your core life and financial values. Below is a sample list of core values, although there are many other values inventories available online or in books like Dr. Russ Harris' *The Confidence Gap*.[27]

Which values jump off the page for you?

- Accomplishment
- Activity
- Advancement
- Belonging
- Care for the Environment
- Care for Others
- Collaboration
- Compassion
- Connection
- Courage
- Creativity
- Curiosity
- Dependability
- Discipline
- Equality
- Excitement
- Financial Security
- Generosity
- Hard Work
- Health

---

[27] Harris, R. (2011).

- Humility
- Independence
- Learning
- Originality
- Patience
- Power
- Privacy
- Relationships
- Reliability
- Reputation

- Resilience
- Responsibility
- Risk-Taking
- Security
- Spirituality
- Success
- Tradition
- Trust
- Wealth

Another way to identify your values is to become mindful of your own behavior and choices.

For example, a value like "connection" can mean different things to different people. If you're given a choice between spending time with a small group of friends or attending a large gathering, a person who values close relationships might choose the smaller gathering, while a person who values having a large network might choose the larger. Both people value connection—they just experience connection differently.

When it comes to your finances, a person who believes in living for today might choose to spend more on their wants, while a person who has the value of strong financial security might choose to save more money.

As you move through your day and make similar decisions, ask yourself what values you base your choices on.

Our values shape our lives, whether or not we are conscious of them. Becoming more aware of our values helps us to better identify and articulate what kind of lives we want to live—and set the goals that help us get there.

Goals are an indispensable part of life, and of retirement planning.

Why Set Goals?

According to researchers Edward Locke and Gary Latham, goals improve our behavior and our performance, and help us figure out how to direct and focus our energy.[28] As you might have experienced in your own life, setting a goal and working toward that goal can be a major source of motivation.

Goals provide incredible psychological benefits as well, by helping us focus on what's important.

Think back to a time when you wanted to achieve something, whether that was beating the previous quarter's sales or running a half-marathon, and how it felt to prioritize your activities to achieve that goal.

It feels good! Even when that goal represents a source of external accomplishment, the psychological benefits are real.

Having a goal in mind also improves performance, and the more specific you get with your goals, the better you will perform.[29] Part of the reason for this is that setting challenging goals creates a personal expectation that we'll meet the goal.

If we expect ourselves to meet the goal, we're more likely to put in the work towards it. We wind up feeling more satisfied with our lives when we are meeting that expectation.

Setting a goal creates the conditions necessary for the behavior, performance, and motivation needed to achieve the goal. Goals help you focus your energy and live without regret.

I saw this play out with some of my clients, a couple named Rosa and Benjamin. Ben and Rosa were wondering if it would be possible for them to retire with a $2 million portfolio. As we walked through their goals, I asked about what role charitable giving would play. Rosa, who had been relatively quiet until that point, spoke up and said that giving to charity was important to her.

---

[28] Locke, E. A., Latham, G.P., Smith, K. J., and Wood, R. E. (1990).
[29] Latham, G. P. (2004).

Through the conversation, I discovered that Rosa wanted to prioritize charitable giving while she and Ben were still alive, whereas Ben had been more inclined to leave money to charities at the end of their lives. Ben didn't have a strong opinion on that strategy, however, so we looked at how the couple could feel more confident about retiring and understand how much they could give away each year.

In analyzing their portfolio, I found that they had a slightly concentrated position in one stock. It was only about 15% of their portfolio, but the appreciated securities would come with a hefty capital gains tax.

The strategy we came up with—contributing that stock to a donor-advised fund—allowed us to achieve multiple goals at once:

- Increasing Ben and Rosa's feelings of relaxed confidence in their retirement plan

- Enabling Rosa to enact her value of charitable giving and set specific goals for each year's donations

- Engaging Rosa more deeply in the financial planning activities

- De-risking the portfolio by reducing the concentrated position

- Avoiding capital gains tax by contributing the securities to the donor-advised fund

- Maximizing Ben and Rosa's tax deduction

Donor-advised funds are amazing tools, and we'll talk more about them in Chapter Ten. The point here, however, is that by focusing on values and goals, Ben and Rosa were able to create a financial plan that benefited multiple parts of their financial life.

As Lindsay Tigar wrote, the simple act of setting goals comes with benefits.[30] Our productivity improves, we feel more satisfied, and we gain perspective. Goals direct our attention and give us clarity on what's important, in work and in life.

When it comes to planning for retirement, it's essential to have goals in mind. Creating goals for your retirement nest egg and your spending activities will determine your priorities now and in the future.

In the next sections, we'll talk about some frameworks, strategies, and benchmarks that can help with retirement planning.

The Four Retirements

Before we get into any specific goal-setting activities for retirement planning, it's important to connect your values to the type of retirement you want to have—or are already having!

While those of us who've worked in consulting might roll our eyes at the idea of another 2x2 diagram, the following 2x2 neatly sums up the four options you likely have for retirement:

	SPEND LESS	SPEND MORE
RETIRE SOONER	*1* FIRE	*4* DYNAMIC
RETIRE LATER	*2* CONSERVATIVE	*3* TRADITIONAL

The first option requires you to spend less but allows you to retire

---

[30] Tigar, L. (2020).

sooner. The most extreme form of this type of retirement has taken shape in the FIRE movement, where FIRE stands for Financial Independence, Retire Early.

FIRE proponents, like Pete Adeney of Mr. Money Mustache,[31] show how dramatically reduced spending and radically increased saving and investing can enable people to opt for an early retirement. FIRE is an attractive path for individuals who value freedom and frugality.

The second option is a conservative one: you can spend less and retire later. While you might not reduce your spending to the level of some FIRE aficionados, many people who choose the conservative path want to have a truly immense nest egg when they reach traditional retirement age.

The conservative option allows you to increase your spending in retirement, thanks to the frugality employed during the wealth-building years. This path is especially appealing for those who value financial security.

The third option is the most traditional: spend more and retire later. In this option, you might choose to follow all the usual retirement advice, such as maxing out your 401(k), getting the company match, using individual retirement accounts, and investing wisely. You spend comfortably along the way and retire at a traditional age. This path is ideal for those who value predictability.

Finally, you can choose to spend more and retire sooner, but you'll have to have a riskier portfolio and a retirement plan that may require you to make big spending cuts at times.

This final, dynamic retirement option relies on having a robust pile of cash and an extremely flexible approach to your retirement portfolio, as well as the option to un-retire should your financial situation or the market become truly dire. The dynamic path is intriguing for those who value excitement and risk.

The thing to keep in mind is that there's no one right path to take;

---

[31] Adeney, P. (2021).

there is just the path that's right for *you*.

Once you have examined the available options and connected those options to your values, you can start thinking about whether your portfolio and spending habits are aligned with your goals.

Setting SMART Goals

Having goals is an important part of achieving a sense of relaxed confidence in retirement—setting and hitting your targets is a great way to know you're on track for the type of retirement lifestyle you want.

Setting and working towards specific goals is, as mentioned above, helpful for increasing the likelihood that you meet those goals.

Financial goals provide you direction when it comes to all your spending, saving, and investing activities. Financial goals also improve your performance because setting goals increases the motivation for working towards them.

As with all other goals, it can be helpful to have a guide. You can translate your life goals into financial goals, and you can do this by adopting the SMART goal framework. SMART goals have been around since the 1980s, but they're just as relevant now as they were back then. A SMART goal is one that is Specific, Measurable, Achievable, Relevant/Realistic, and Time-Bound.

A SMART goal is much more likely to be achieved than a vague wish because the SMART framework gets you to think through all aspects of how you'll work towards the goal. In the example below, we explore how to take a vague goal—like "becoming a better photographer"—through the SMART goal process.

When it comes to your retirement planning, SMART goals are critical. "I want to have a comfortable retirement" is a nice-sounding goal, but like becoming a better photographer, it's too vague to be useful.

Say, for example, one of your goals is to become a better photographer. That's an admirable goal, but it's too vague to be achievable.

Instead, you might set a Specific and Realistic goal of having your photography accepted for display in a local coffee shop or art gallery by the end of the year, which also makes the goal Time-Bound. You can make this goal more Achievable by signing up for a course with a professional photographer, and Measure progress by getting feedback and setting aside 30 minutes a day to work on your photography skills.

NERDING OUT!

Instead, your goal might be:

- Specific: Retiring with $3 million in your portfolio.

- Measurable: You know the exact gap between your current portfolio and the portfolio you want to have at retirement.

- Achievable: After examining your current income and investment activities, you know exactly what you need to set aside each year to hit that target.

- Realistic: You are already on your way to that $3 million rather than starting from scratch.

- Time-Bound: You want to retire within 10 years.

When it comes to your retirement planning, SMART goals are helpful because you can introduce different dollar amounts, goal priorities, and timelines. You can modify the SMART goal framework above to match your own goals and circumstances and see a step-by-step plan begin to form.

Goal-setting is an important part of life personally, professionally, and financially.

Thinking about retirement doesn't mean you never stop setting goals for yourself—just that the goals will start to look a bit different.

Back of Your Napkin Math (The 4% Rule)

As you identify your values and start thinking about your retirement planning goals, it also helps to get a rough idea of what your spending capacity will be in retirement.

In the 1980s, a CFP named Bill Bengen came up with what is commonly called the 4% Rule, which helps individuals start to quantify their spending based on their portfolio.[32] The 4% Rule was further elaborated on in 1998 in a paper that is now nicknamed the Trinity Study.[33]

The study is based on a few key assumptions:

1. Your portfolio consists of the S&P 500 and U.S. Treasury bonds. Your allocation in the S&P 500 ranges from 50% to 75%

2. There is a 30-year time horizon

3. The 4% withdrawal rate is based on the starting value of the portfolio and increased to match inflation each year

What Bengen and the authors of the Trinity Study all found (based on back testing only) is that you can safely withdraw 4% each year (again, adjusted for inflation)—no matter what ends up going on with the performance of the portfolio—and never run out of money. All sorts of people have come up with refinements over time, but the 4% rule continues to be a classic and conservative approach.[34]

Let's look at an example of how this might work in practice.

Say you have a portfolio worth $3 million across all your accounts. A safe withdrawal rate of 4% means you can safely withdraw $120,000 in year one, or $10,000 per month. If inflation is 3% in year 2, then that $120,000 increases to $123,600—even if the value of the portfolio has fallen significantly! You should be able to withdraw $10,000 per month with confidence.

That's not a bad deal!

[32] Arends, B. (2020).
[33] Cooley, P. L., Hubbard, C. M., Walz, D. T. (1998).
[34] Arends, B. (2020).

Let's say you have an additional $60,000 per year in Social Security benefits on top of your individual portfolio. That means you wind up with $180,000 of income in year one! Even assuming 20% goes to taxes, that leaves you with $144,000 of spending capacity each year, or $12,000 each month.

That $120,000 or $144,000 can then be broken down into categories. You can make this breakdown by identifying your non-negotiable monthly or annual expenses. Always make sure your non-negotiable expenses are covered first. Everything that's left can then be put towards fun spending, donations, and other activities.

The 4% Rule is a starting point for many investors who want to figure out how much of their portfolio they can safely withdraw and offers a top-down perspective on your retirement spending capabilities. Some investors choose to lean more conservatively with their money and withdraw only 3% or 3.5%, while others use Bengen's newer 4.5% or 5% withdrawal rate.

The key benefit of applying the 4% rule is that it can further assist you in setting SMART goals for your retirement planning. Once you have employed the 4% rule to get a rough sense of your spending capacity, you can start to break that number down into relevant categories that are aligned with your values.

Needs, Wants, and Wishes

I encourage you to further organize your financial and retirement goals into three categories, which we'll call Needs, Wants, and Wishes. These categories roughly align with Maslow's hierarchy of needs, including our basic psychological and safety needs all the way through our wishes for self-actualization and leaving a legacy. [35]

Separating your goals by category will help you identify key priorities, notice any conflicts or risk areas before they pose a real problem, and provide you with clear targets for each area of your life.

---

[35] McLeod, S. (2020).

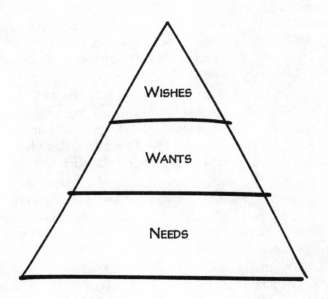

Let's break down Needs, Wants, and Wishes a bit further:

- **Needs** are non-discretionary spending categories.
  - o Your Needs include basic living expenses and healthcare costs—the non-negotiable spending required to get through life. No matter what happens, you must be able to afford your Needs for the rest of your life. No question.

- **Wants** are plans for discretionary spending categories like buying a vacation home, traveling, or paying for your grandkids' education.
  - o Your Wants are things that, if there is a massive stock market crash and no recovery in sight, could be dialed back: Instead of taking that 3-week trip to Barcelona, you schedule a 1-week trip to Miami.

- **Wishes** are the long-term legacy-focused spending and giving categories that you'll only be able to afford if the stock market behaves.
  - Your Wishes are things like leaving a million dollars to your kids or your alma mater. It's great to have these goals in mind when you plan, and it's much easier to identify what your Wishes are if you know your values.

Needs, Wants, and Wishes interact with one another. Your Needs form the foundation of your financial plan, the basis from which all other spending is made possible.

Without covering your Needs, there is no possibility of reaching your Wants or your Wishes—but there are ways to make it all happen. We'll see in upcoming chapters how this comes together.

Setting goals for your Needs, Wants, and Wishes serves as a framework for all your financial decision-making about retirement. Developing SMART goals will also show you how you can meet Specific, Measurable, Achievable, Relevant/Realistic, and Time-Bound goals in each category.

Conclusions

Setting goals is important—both in life and in our finances. Goals that are rooted in our values direct our behavior and help us improve, and the more specific you can be when setting your goals, the better. When it comes to financial planning, your goals should be shaped by your values, your spending plans, and your retirement timeline.

Additionally, you'll want to think about the relationship between your goals, your need, ability, and willingness to bear risk, your income floor, your portfolio, and your tax burden. These more detailed financial planning topics are the subjects of the coming chapters.

Throughout the rest of this book, you'll learn more about how to cultivate a feeling of relaxed confidence in retirement through financial planning.

Key Takeaways

- **Values:** Principles that shape how we make decisions and find meaning in life. Our values should inform our life goals and our financial goals.

- Goals improve our behavior and our performance. Goals help us to focus and direct our energy.

- There are four potential approaches to retirement that will influence the types of financial goals you set:

o   FIRE: Spend less, retire sooner

o   Conservative: Spend less, retire later

o   Traditional: Spend more, retire later

o   Dynamic: Spend more, retire sooner

- The SMART goal framework is useful for setting financial goals:

  o   S: Specific

  o   M: Measurable

  o   A: Achievable

  o   R: Realistic/Relevant

  o   T: Time-Bound

- The 4% rule says you can safely withdraw 4% of your portfolio each year (adjusted for inflation) and never run out of money.

- There are three major categories of retirement spending to consider when setting goals:

  o   **Needs:** Non-discretionary, non-negotiable spending (food, housing, medical care)

  o   **Wants:** Discretionary spending (travel, vacation home, funding education expenses for grandchildren)

  o   **Wishes:** Long-term legacy spending and donations (leaving $1 million to your alma mater, your heirs, or a charity)

- Your financial goals should be grounded in your values and aligned with your approach to retirement, your level of spending in retirement, and your Needs, Wants, and Wishes.

5. Building Your Financial Resilience

Like many people, I learned about the importance of resilience the hard way.

As described earlier, I spent the first 38 years of my life feeling confident, racking up achievements, and paying no attention to resilience. Why would I? Everything was going well for me.

When my confidence came crashing down, I wasn't equipped to deal with the shock of it. I didn't have the resilience I needed to deal with those challenges.

I've been thinking about, and working on, building, and maintaining resilience ever since.

Resilience is the psychological ability to cope with a crisis or recover from difficulty. You can think of it as a form of mental elasticity: the more resilient you are, the quicker you'll bounce back.

Resilience does not mean you'll never experience anything difficult—we all face challenges. What resilience does is help you cope more readily with those difficulties when they inevitably arise.

The great thing about resilience is that, like optimism and confidence, it's not an inherent personality trait available to only those lucky enough to be born with it. You can learn resilience.

A big part of resilience involves learning healthy ways of thinking about risk. For example: Rebuilding my confidence required me to stop ruminating on potential catastrophes, which was keeping me locked in a state of constant worry. Instead, I learned how to be more resilient, and to pair the power of catastrophic thinking with optimism and confidence.

So far, we've covered the importance of confidence, optimism, and values-driven goals for your financial plan. We've discussed how to identify your Needs, Wants, and Wishes, and to align them with your goals.

In this chapter, we're going to dive a little further into thinking about your retirement financial plan and the role resilience plays in it.

While psychological resilience is an important individual capacity to develop, it's also critical to think about the resilience of your financial plan. Resilience has a similar connotation here: How quickly can your plan bounce back after a challenge like a market drop?

It's time to start thinking about the financial risks you'll likely face in retirement and *building resilience into your financial plan from the ground up.*

Enter The Chief Risk Officer

During my career, I spent a bit of time working in the burgeoning field of data privacy. The internet has ushered in all sorts of concerns and risks as companies try to protect user information—and their own data, to boot.

Chief Risk Officers across the country were starting to manage privacy risk, so I also learned what Chief Risk Officers do, how they operate, and how they think.

In the traditional corporate setting, the Chief Risk Officer is responsible for identifying, analyzing, and addressing potential threats to the company. The threats can be internal or external. They can come from technical issues, regulatory changes, or competition. They might also involve physical risks, threats to profitability, and more.

The Chief Risk Officer's first task is to build out a complete **risk register**, or a list of potential risks. Once the Chief Risk Officer has cataloged every possible risk, then and only then can they take a step back, examine the list dispassionately, and start making recommendations about the appropriate course of action.

A risk register, like the one included here, can be as simple as a table identifying the risk, its likelihood, its potential impact and severity, and what action should be taken.

Description	Eaten by Shark	Killed by Heart Disease
Likelihood	Remote Chance (1 in 4.3 million)	Decent Chance (1 in 5)
Impact	Death	Death
Severity	Extreme	Extreme
Strategy	**ASSUME the risk** (go swimming)	**MITIGATE the risk** (adopt a healthy lifestyle)

NERDING OUT!

It's easy to think that we must leap into action the second we've identified a risk—but nothing could be further from the truth.

Some risks or the actions we take to deal with those risks will interact with each other. The Chief Risk Officer's role is not just identifying the risks, but looking for potential interactions, assessing and analyzing probabilities, and choosing the course of action that leads to the best possible outcome.

In other words, the Chief Risk Officer must have the skills to think catastrophically—in a productive way! This is key to creating a financial plan that has resilience built in.

Only after developing and assessing the risk register can the Chief Risk Officer articulate sound strategies for dealing with potential risks. There are four choices: the Chief Risk Officer can make recommendations that **avoid, assume, mitigate, or transfer** risk.

AVOID	ASSUME
MITIGATE	TRANSFER

Such choices might include changing a business policy to align with new laws, thus avoiding a penalty. Assuming risk might involve setting aside funds in case of a negative outcome. The Chief Risk Officer might recommend mitigating risk by developing a new safety plan that reduces the risk of worker injury. Transferring the risk might look like purchasing insurance to guard against financial losses.

The ultimate goal of any of these four choices is creating an organization that is resilient in the face of setbacks. Rather than scrambling to respond to catastrophe once it's already struck, a Chief

Risk Officer helps their organization create a risk register, plan for negative outcomes, and then work towards positive ones.

There's a lot the Chief Risk Officer can teach us about risk and resilience in our own retirement financial plans.

Let's briefly consider the choices you have when it comes to risk:

1. **Avoid:** Avoiding risk entails making a change that eliminates or significantly reduces the chances that the risk will come to pass. You can avoid the risk of your company's stock tanking by selling it, or by having it occupy only a small percentage of your overall holdings.

2. **Assume:** Assuming risk involves making financial or other preparations for absorbing the cost of the risk. You can assume the risk of investing in the stock market, as almost all of us do during our wealth-building years.

3. **Mitigate:** Mitigating risk means offsetting the risk through actions that will reduce its impact. You can mitigate the risk of inflation by deferring Social Security to age 70, since Social Security is inflation-protected, and the benefits increase over 8% for every year of deferral.

4. **Transfer:** Transferring risk involves paying someone else to cover the cost of the risk. You can transfer the risk of a massive long-term healthcare bill to an insurance company, which is set up to pool risk.

As a financial advisor, thinking about financial risk from the perspective of a Chief Risk Officer was a major lightbulb moment for me. I'd assumed I was in the wealth management business, and that my services were solely focused on investment and financial planning—but what if I had been thinking about it all wrong?

What if what people really needed was someone to...

- Play the Chief Risk Officer role for their financial lives,

- Develop their risk register and think broadly about those risks, and

- Help them make the best possible choices?

The Chief Risk Officer role is one you can take on yourself, but it's also a great role to outsource. Let someone else do the catastrophic thinking for you, so you can focus on enjoying the outcome: a financial plan that inspires confidence and optimism, and that is already built to be resilient to financial shocks.

Investment management and financial planning come with risks! Even if you're fully invested in Vanguard funds or feel like your financial plan is solid, there are risks that could upset your ability to carry your plan to fruition.

Knowing what those risks are and how to respond to them is essential for developing a retirement financial plan that is resilient enough to still function when difficulties arise.

Risk is part of every investment strategy, financial plan, and life itself. Ruminating, or constantly focusing on risk, is a great way to make yourself anxious and paranoid rather than relaxed and confident. However, it's just as dangerous to bury your head in the sand and ignore risk.

Neither rumination nor naïve optimism promotes psychological resilience in the long run. Ruminating drains your energy and pretending risk doesn't exist leaves you totally unprepared when a challenge does appear—and it will.

Practicing good risk management means taking the time to acknowledge potential risks and pitfalls, coming up with contingency plans for each item on your risk register, and then enjoying the feeling of relaxed confidence that comes from knowing you and your financial plan are built to be resilient.

Rather than constantly focusing on risk or ignoring it until catastrophe strikes, you can learn how to identify risks, make plans, and then stop worrying!

Clever insurance agents have long tried to equate "risk management" with "purchasing an insurance policy"—ideally from that agent. No, no, no. A thousand times no!

Risk management needs to become a much broader concept in your financial life. Buying insurance is transferring risk—but remember that it is only one of the strategies you can employ. Be sure to consider all available options before handing over your hard-earned money to a slick insurance salesperson.

Start by building out a risk register of each major financial risk you face, examine your risks as a group, and *then* decide which of the strategies to apply to each one!

Back to Resilience

Instead of filling the Chief Risk Officer role in your financial life, I'm going to argue that you should think of it as the Chief *Resilience* Officer role. I strongly prefer this way of thinking because it is far less cold and clinical. It is far more personal and evokes all the attributes of resilience that I mentioned above.

Someone once told me that "personal finance is 80% personal and 20% finance," and creating your own Chief Resilience Officer acknowledges that fact.

It's entirely possible to build out a financial plan by prioritizing your goals, adding up your resources, and then designing a portfolio that aligns with your goals. That's a great start—but it isn't the whole picture. There's another step to take to make sure your plan is resilient.

Once you've created the plan, you need to absolutely hammer that plan with potential threats.

This process will help you understand whether your financial plan has enough resilience to withstand difficulties. It will also show you if there are specific risks your plan is resilient to, and if there are areas of weakness.

Now, I enjoyed statistics—but my friend Larry paid more attention than I did. When I was thinking about risks, I turned to him with a question. Let's say you already know you face nine potential catastrophic risks—risks that put your entire plan in jeopardy—and the chance of any one of those risks hitting is about 7%. How do you know what to plan for? How do you get a true sense of the risks you face?

Larry, still being great with statistics, wrote a combinatorics program to calculate some odds for us. It turns out this sort of inclusion-exclusion problem produces some interesting results!

- The chance of 0 significant risks hitting is 47%.

That means 47 out of 100 retirees are in the clear! That's almost 50/50 odds—not bad. That means you'll likely wind up slightly overprepared for risks in retirement, which is a great way to increase your feelings of relaxed confidence.

- The chance of one major risk hitting is 37%.

Another 37 retirees only have to deal with one major risk coming to pass. That's still not bad! The tricky part, of course, is that it's impossible to know ahead of time which risk it might be. We'll talk below about how to intelligently prepare for the nine potential risks you might face.

- The chance of two catastrophic risks hitting is 13%.

About 13 retirees are going to face two or more risks coming to fruition. If you've been preparing for risks in retirement, odds are you're going to be able to weather this without too much trouble.

- The chance of three large-scale risks hitting is 3%.

An unlucky three retirees will have three major risks hit during their retirement years—whether that's all at once or across decades. While the odds of this happening are low, they're not nonexistent. We'll talk later on in this chapter about what I call the Katrina Protocols: a backup plan for if the worst really does come to pass.

In general, the best way to figure out how to prepare for potential risks is to test your financial plan with an advisor who uses Monte Carlo simulations to understand a wide range of portfolio possibilities.

Once you've run the tests, maybe you discover your existing plan is resilient in seven of the nine risks. That's a great result, *and* you walk away from the exercise knowing to focus your attention on the other risks!

The point is not to have you start ruminating about potential risks or catastrophes that could strike your retirement financial plan. That will just lead to anxiety, and not the feeling of relaxed confidence I want you to retire with.

Instead, focus your attention on the remaining risks and then come up with an action plan for avoiding, assuming, mitigating, or transferring each risk. Building resilience into your retirement plan requires you to acknowledge that some unknown number of bad things *could* happen. It doesn't mean they all will, but you can count on the possibility of some of them coming to fruition.

The difficulty, of course, is that there's no real way to predict which will happen and which won't. Knowing what the risks are allows you to come up with an approach that increases resilience.

You can cultivate your own powers of resilience by focusing on your confidence, your optimism, and your overall mindset. We'll continue discussing these topics throughout the rest of the book.

You can also create resilience in your financial plan by employing strategies that will address the most significant risks you're likely to face. The rest of this chapter explores some of those risks in detail.

Risk #1: The Stock Market Might Collapse

What happens if the stock market collapses—like, really collapses? I think that in recent decades we've been lulled into thinking that stocks aren't all that risky.

In our lifetimes, the stock market has bounced back pretty quickly from every drop and every course correction. Even the big ones have ended relatively quickly, compared to past recessions and depressions. This has not always been the case, and it certainly hasn't been the case in other countries.

Stocks are risky, and it's possible they won't cooperate during your retirement. Fortunately, the next chapters cover exactly what you need to know to have a resilient retirement financial plan.

Chapter Six describes how to build an income floor that will meet your Needs for life, and Chapters Seven, Eight, and Nine create a big-picture view of investing and wealth management.

Even if the stock market takes a long-term tumble, you'll have a resilient financial plan in place. The strategies described in the next several chapters help mitigate the risk to your investments, even though they don't erase them entirely.

Risk #2: You Might Retire into the Start of a Brutal Bear Market

There is a subtle, but important, distinction between the risk of stock market returns being less than expected and the sequence of those returns. The stock market has historically returned 10%.[36]

Let's say that continues for the rest of your life. Sounds good, right?

---

[36] Royal, J. and O'Shea, A. (2021).

Not necessarily. If you are unlucky and retire into a protracted bear market, your portfolio might get whacked so hard (because the market does poorly *and* you are withdrawing money) that it could be too late for the ensuing bull market to make much of a difference.

This is the sequence of returns risk, which is described in more detail in Chapter Six. You can declaw sequence of returns risk by building out your income floor.

Another way to mitigate sequence of returns risk is to be prepared to pull back on some of your Wants and Wishes spending if necessary.

Risk #3: Inflation Might Surge

When I started writing this book, the big worry was that we hadn't had bad inflation since the 1970s—but what if it came back?

The COVID-19 pandemic and its economic impacts had many financial analysts speculating about the possibility of increasing inflation.[37] By the time I finished writing the book, inflation had in fact increased significantly and rapidly.

High inflation erodes purchasing power, and it can put parts of your financial plan at risk, as many people found out the hard way in the late spring of 2022.

Inflation can hit retirees particularly hard. Most corporate pensions are not adjusted for inflation, and those that are generally cap the increases. Income annuities, likewise, do not adjust for inflation. Bonds don't fare well against high inflation either, and many retirees prefer to take a hefty slug of bonds.

But here's the thing: Even as I write this, it's still impossible to see the future. Will inflation continue to increase, or will it fall again? How long will high inflation last?

---

[37] Carosa, C. (2021).

No one can say for sure, which means my advice in this section doesn't actually change. We can't predict the future; we *can* make plans that protect our finances, regardless of what inflation does.

The good news is that stocks and real estate have always been good inflation hedges. Your diversified investment portfolio and any investment property you own will automatically act to minimize the impact that inflation might have on your finances.

Taking stock of your stocks and devoting part of your portfolio to investing in real estate can help keep you on track for the lifestyle you want, even if the economy experiences inflation.

There are some government bonds with built-in inflation protection: iBonds adjust their interest rates based on inflation, although there are currently significant limitations on how much you can invest each year. Treasury Inflation Protected Securities (TIPS) are another option. If you are convinced inflation will take off, these securities are a good option—but if inflation does not pick up, the returns are poor.

Another strategy you can use to avoid the potential impact of inflation on your spending power is deferring Social Security until 70. This deferral provides significant protection against inflation because you'll receive a much larger monthly payment.

Starting your benefit at 70 results in a 77% increase in your payments, versus taking it at 62. So if you tap your portfolio to help you defer until 70, you'll end up with a much stronger hedge against inflation because the federal government is increasing your payment so significantly. This strategy is especially useful for protecting your income floor and ensuring your Needs will always be met.

Some people focus on gold as an inflation hedge, but the evidence for its effectiveness is mixed—at best. There are also costs (and opportunity costs) to holding gold over opting for the other strategies discussed throughout this book.

I believe that making sure your balance sheet includes a good amount of both real estate and stocks and deferring Social Security until 70 (for the higher-earning spouse, if you're married) is sufficient for hedging against inflation for most people.

Risk #4: Income Interruptus

If you're already retired, you have completed the process of exchanging your human capital for financial capital. Since the role of life and disability insurance is to protect human capital from catastrophic financial loss, you no longer have an insurable need.

If you're still working, and especially if you have more than a couple years to go and/or you are making a lot of money, then premature death should be on your risk register. Dying before retirement leaves your surviving spouse or dependents in the lurch, especially if the long-term financial plan rests primarily on your income.

Most people I talk to have done a nice job on the life insurance front, and generally opt for term life insurance, which is excellent. Run for the hills if someone tries to sell you a permanent life insurance policy (while there are exceptions, they are rare).

However, it is still worth seeing if you have a gap. For example, if you make $500,000 a year and have 10 years until retirement but only carry $2 million in term life insurance, you might have a gap.

A new client of mine, Sandra, lost her husband unexpectedly. She has two teenage children and limited earning power of her own. As a result of this sudden loss, Sandra was—understandably—dealing with significant financial uncertainty and anxiety. Fortunately, we were able to build a plan that clarified her new "spending guardrails" to keep her and her family on track.

At the end of our last meeting, she told me she was no longer worried. Many people fail to plan for an early death, leaving their grieving families to search for a way back to financial security. Planning for this risk, even while hoping it never comes to pass, is one way to protect yourself and your loved ones from financial insecurity.

In addition to the risk of early death, disability can also be tricky. Think about the airbag effect, or the fact that we have gotten really, really good at keeping people alive even in a catastrophic event like a major car accident.

The airbag effect increases the relevance of long-term disability insurance (LTDI) because even though we're better at saving lives, there are often lifelong issues that result from major illness or accidents.

LTDI can be confusing and expensive. Most people are uncomfortable with thinking about the possibility of becoming disabled, and so choose to live with the gap—and the financial consequences.

It doesn't have to be this way. Instead, think about this risk like a CRO to decide what you would do if the risk came to pass. If you identify a gap, investigate a supplemental LTDI policy, assuming you already have basic coverage through work.

Risk #5: Superannuation

Many of us actually underestimate how long we'll live.[38] You and your spouse might both live for a long, long time!

In this case, you need to ensure that your retirement financial plan can cover your Needs should you live to be, say, 95 or 100. Stress testing your retirement plan will come in handy here as well.

As we will discuss in Chapter Six, **longevity risk** is the risk of outliving your money. The longer you live, the greater your longevity risk becomes. Fortunately, it's possible to transfer longevity risk to an insurance company by purchasing an income annuity.

You can also mitigate longevity risk by taking the monthly payments from a company pension rather than a lump sum buyout. Monthly pension payments last for life, meaning you will have a steady, reliable source of income no matter what.

Deferring Social Security payments to age 70 also increases your monthly benefit to the maximum level. As Social Security is another benefit you cannot outlive, this deferral also helps mitigate longevity risk.

---

[38] Botella, E. (2019).

Risk #6: Long-Term Care Shock

You or your spouse might find yourselves in a nursing home or assisted living facility. Long-term care is a medical expense that is not currently covered under Medicare.

You need to know whether your financial plan will survive a stretch of long-term care.

If you ask a broker who the ideal candidate for long-term care insurance is, it's someone between 50 and 64 years old with a $1-4 million portfolio. Here's why: if you have more than $4 million, you can self-insure. If you have less than $1 million, you probably can't afford the insurance. If you're over 64, the cost of the insurance is wildly expensive—and if you're under 50, you wind up paying for insurance you may never use.

A recent Genworth Cost of Care Survey found that 70% of people will need long-term care at some point in their lives.[39] The same survey showed that a private room in a nursing home costs an average of $290 per day—that adds up to more than $100,000 a year!

Such an increase in necessary spending can quickly deplete your financial reserves if you haven't planned for it.

So how do you know whether long-term care insurance is the right decision? That's the question that two of my clients had. At first glance, the Fishers and the Elliotts seemed quite similar: each couple was between 50 and 64 years old and had a portfolio comfortably in the $1-4 million range.

Yet the Fishers decided to buy it, and the Elliotts did not. What was the difference? It all came down to the resources each couple had in the event the risk came to pass. The Elliotts had a $2 million buffer asset in the form of their home, which they could draw on should either of them ever need long-term care. The Fishers also had a buffer asset in their home—but that buffer asset was only worth $300,000.

---

[39] Genworth (2021).

When we ran simulations, the need for long-term care didn't materially impact the Elliotts' plan; they could essentially self-insure. The need for long-term care had a major impact on the Fishers' retirement plan, so purchasing insurance made sense.

Once again, you'll want to run the numbers on how this expense will affect your own retirement financial plan. You may be able to self-insure for long-term care costs, meaning you'll simply assume the expense should you need to. However, you might also decide to transfer the cost by purchasing long-term care insurance.

Risk #7: Lending an (Unplanned) Hand

One of the first questions I ask my clients is, "Who should be in your financial plan?"

I usually get one of two answers: "Just the two of us," from clients whose children are grown, or "The two of us and our kids," from clients whose children are still in school (including college).

Many of my clients plan to help their kids graduate from college, pay for weddings, and maybe provide a down payment for their kids' first home. Then they plan to spend on themselves for the rest of their lives.

That seems like it makes sense—but sometimes things don't work out that way.

Sometimes, something unplanned happens:

- A parent needs long-term care (in their own home or in a facility), and they don't have long-term care insurance.

- A child gets into an accident, or struggles with a mental health concern, and can't work. They need financial assistance to get back on their feet.

- A grandchild is diagnosed with autism and needs coaching and assistance at a walk-in center that isn't covered by insurance and is otherwise out of reach financially.

You might, unexpectedly or not, find yourself needing to provide financial support for a parent, child, grandchild, sibling, or other relative. Financial support might include covering a range of unexpected costs—and those costs can be high.

You need to know whether your financial plan can weather a period of higher-than-expected expenses if you find yourself with unplanned financial responsibility. Running a simulation on your financial plan can help you determine whether your retirement funds can withstand these extra expenses.

Risk #8: You Might Get Sued

We live in a litigious society. If you hit the wrong person's car, they might not be content with letting the insurance companies work it out, and you could get sued.

There are any number of reasons—frivolous or not—that you may wind up in court. Hiring an attorney and dealing with court costs is expensive. This risk requires you to think about the necessity of asset protection.

There are two primary strategies you can use to protect your assets: you can transfer the risk to an insurance provider, or you can place your assets within an irrevocable trust.

Asset Protection: Purchase Umbrella Liability Insurance

If you decide to transfer your risk to an insurance company, you'll want to seek out umbrella liability insurance. Make sure your umbrella liability policy is large enough to protect the bulk of your net worth.

An umbrella insurance policy is personal liability insurance that fills in once you have hit your insurance liability limit for homeowner, auto, or other types of insurance, and protects your assets in the event of a lawsuit. If someone sues you successfully, the court can order that a portion of your income be garnished.

Imagine, for example, that you are found to be at fault for a serious car accident that damaged multiple other vehicles and caused major injuries, and you're ordered to pay $1 million in total damages.

Even if you have the highest possible deductible on your auto insurance, most auto insurance companies' accident liability tops out at $300,000-$500,000. You'll be left holding the bag for $500,000-$700,000 of damages—and that money will come from your retirement fund.

However, if you have a $1 million umbrella insurance policy, your own assets will be protected, and the insurance company will pay the remaining costs.

The benefits of umbrella insurance are that the policies are typically inexpensive, and they provide peace of mind across the board for unforeseen legal problems. You can transfer the risk of getting entangled in unexpected legal battles to an insurance company with the knowledge that your assets will be protected.

Asset Protection: Set Up an Irrevocable Trust

Another method of protecting your assets is to set up an irrevocable trust. Money in a retirement account or irrevocable trust is often (though not always) protected from lawsuits; money in the bank and in taxable investment accounts is at risk.

A revocable trust, sometimes called a living trust, is a type of trust that you can change or even cancel. This type of trust does not protect your assets!

An irrevocable trust, on the other hand, does. An irrevocable trust cannot be changed or canceled once you've signed the document. In essence, it builds a moat around any assets that you put into the trust.

This type of trust creates a unique tax entity that you no longer control—which means, in the event of a lawsuit, those assets are untouchable. The downside, of course, is that you pay for the trust's creation and management, and you sacrifice some freedom and flexibility when it comes to your finances.

Most people would rather purchase affordable umbrella insurance and retain control over their money, but it's important to know that irrevocable trusts are also an option. Protecting your assets is the goal; the specific tactic you choose to do so depends on your preferences.

Risk #9: You Might Experience Cognitive Decline

We all tend to experience some cognitive decline as we age, but, like long-term disability, it's not something most of us like to think about.

Cognitive decline can have a negative impact on your overall well-being as well as your finances, especially if you lose the ability to manage your money. Fortunately, there are several ways to mitigate this risk.

From an individual perspective, health-related behaviors like eating well and getting enough sleep, staying mentally engaged, maintaining strong social bonds, and participating in physical activity all help to mitigate cognitive decline.[40] Activities like puzzles and games, volunteering, gardening, walking, and visits with friends and family are all ways to keep your mind sharp well into your later years.

Fortunately, you're already on the way to setting up a retirement plan that will allow you to do all those things and more.

As we'll discuss in the coming chapters, building an income floor and a robust and diversified investment plan positions you to live the

---

[40] Jones, J. (2021).

kind of rich and fulfilling life that also will help mitigate the risk of cognitive decline.

From a financial planning perspective, it's also prudent to make sure your finances are as automated as possible.

Simplifying the amount of money management you're required to do will reduce mental strain and, if you do experience some decline, will make it easier for you to continue living comfortably.

You might also consider putting a durable power of attorney in place if you become unable to manage your own finances. A durable power of attorney minimizes the risk of experiencing financial elder abuse, makes your financial plan clear, and ensures you have someone available to help maintain your quality of life.

While it is unpleasant to consider the financial ramifications of severe cognitive decline, it's far better to make plans to mitigate its consequences than to live with those consequences down the line.

You can likely imagine any number of other risks to add to this list. One important part of dealing with risk involves acknowledging that we can't know everything and figuring out how to prepare for disasters we never saw coming.

I Don't Know

One of the strangest things I've experienced in my life is seeing 30 of my fellow Stanford Business School students practicing saying the phrase "I don't know."

The class was called Creativity in Business, and in it we would draw colorful pictures and do all sorts of outside-the-box activities, which admittedly made me think about the $120,000 I was dropping on my MBA—not to mention the two years of lost income.

But still, the most impactful part of the course was the "I don't know" exercise. It was liberating to be able to say the words out loud, and I will never forget the experience. Saying "I don't know" is empowering.

Admitting you don't know something removes the pressure to know everything, and creates the possibility for growth and learning, which is something we'll continue to discuss throughout the book.

When it comes to building resilience in your financial life, you need to lean into "I don't know." We just don't know which risk will actually come to pass, so we need to be prepared for them all.

The odds of each of the risks identified above occurring is, individually, quite small. A small chance that something might occur probably doesn't feel all that significant, especially given everything else that's going on in your life and in the world at large.

However, the odds that at least one of those risks comes to fruition is closer to 100%—and given the nature of the risks, it's possible you'll experience more than one.

This is part of why it's important not to get overly focused on any one risk, especially to the detriment of managing the rest. Examine your risk register like a CRO, and look for potential interactions, as well as the most economical way to address each risk.

It's also important to acknowledge that you can't avoid the risks entirely. There are some risks you shouldn't even try to entirely avoid.

If you decide to transfer some risk to an insurance company, you should only transfer the catastrophic financial risk. In other words, carry the largest deductible you can to lower your premiums. While you will pay the deductible if you need to use the insurance, having lower premiums across all forms of insurance is a better financial bet.

For example, imagine you need long-term care. If you only need a year of care, you can probably pay for it from your portfolio without causing too many problems. If you need five years of long-term care, it's better to have the insurance. It's wise to choose the one-year deductible on the long-term care policy to minimize your premium!

The Katrina Protocols

As we've discussed throughout this chapter, there are a few financial risks you face as you approach retirement. If you address each one of those risks, it's highly likely that your financial plan will be resilient.

But there is always the possibility that we could experience what's known as a "black swan" event. First described by mathematical statistician and former option trader Nassim Taleb, a black swan event is surprising, has a major—often negative—impact, and tends to be rationalized with the benefit of hindsight.[41]

Taleb created the theory to help explain the role of rare events that have a disproportionate impact, the challenge of calculating the odds of such events, and how cognitive biases shape our inability to both predict and react appropriately to black swan events when they do occur.

Let's look at such an event.

The Gulf Coast was hit by terrible storms in 1900 and 1928. In response, the Army Corps of Engineers built 350 miles of levees around New Orleans—an extraordinary feat of engineering that held up beautifully for decades.

Then, in 2005, Hurricane Katrina stuck. The disaster overcame the levees in dozens of places, killed more than 1,200 people, and caused more than $108 billion of devastation. The effects of Hurricane Katrina continue to linger, nearly 20 years after the hurricane itself.

Hurricane Katrina was a black swan event. The impact was significant, surprising, and largely negative; the idea that such a hurricane and such an extent of damage could occur seemed outlandish before it happened; and cognitive biases played a role in shaping the reaction to the event and how it was understood later.

---

[41] Taleb, N. (2007).

After Hurricane Katrina, it was time to think about resilience. Fast forward a few years, and New Orleans had made significant improvements to its hurricane readiness, including adding canals and massive pumps to its infrastructure. While the damage was done, New Orleans is now better prepared to weather the next Katrina.

Consider adding similar Katrina Protocols to your own retirement planning. If you address the major risks you're likely to face in retirement, it is likely that your financial levees will hold up. But you could experience your own black swan event. It's possible, for example, that multiple risks hit at the same time—and hit hard— even if you planned for them.

Articulating your own Katrina Protocols allows you to think catastrophically and design a buffer that you can turn to if the unthinkable comes to pass.

For example, if you own a piece of real estate in addition to your primary residence, this could be an ideal buffer asset in the event of a black swan event. The function of a buffer is to reduce shock or damage—having a buffer asset means you have a little extra cushion if things take a significant downward turn.

You could sell the property, borrow against it, or rent it out when you're not using it. To use an additional piece of real estate as part of your Katrina Protocols, you need to understand three key factors: How much equity do you have in the property? What is fair market value or rent? What is the current occupancy rate?

Another aspect of your Katrina Protocols could be scrapping all Wish spending and curtailing Want spending, at least temporarily. Eliminating Wish spending may be disappointing, but it can help you enhance your ability to absorb an unexpected financial shock.

Cutting Want-related spending is a bit harder: after all, you've worked your whole life to be able to enjoy retirement. Maybe you looked forward to spending $15,000 a year traveling across Europe when suddenly that's not possible due to a need for long-term care, a global pandemic, or some other black swan event.

However, finding ways to reduce your Want spending—at least until you have breathing room again—can make a huge difference for the overall resilience of your plan. Perhaps you spend every other year traveling, instead of every year, or shift a portion of your travel plans to domestic exploration.

A final option for your Katrina Protocols could be converting equity in your home into cashflow, allowing you to stay in your home as long as you want. While many people think of a reverse mortgage as tapping equity to support themselves, several of my clients are starting to think more broadly about how to use a reverse mortgage in the event of a black swan event.

I have a client who owns a total of $16 million worth of real estate across four properties. Everything is completely paid off. Jim has significant spending goals for his retirement, and when we first developed a simulation for his plans, the probability of success came back at 85%. That's not bad, but it wasn't as high as he wanted.

We added another scenario to the planning software that showed a $3 million cash infusion from a private reverse mortgage, which would take effect in 15 years. That cranked the plan's probability of success up to 99%, and helped Jim feel much more confident about his spending goals! He knew that he had a robust buffer asset in case he ever needed it.

Keep in mind that a private jumbo reverse mortgage like this has different requirements than a traditional FHA-backed reverse mortgage, which is stricter—the lending limit is typically a few hundred thousand dollars, based on the property's value and location, any debt you have, and your age. However, even an FHA-backed reverse mortgage can become a lifeline if you experience a black swan event.

One fascinating last note on the Katrina Protocols and the role that a reverse mortgage could play. Some academics are now suggesting that people consider taking out a reverse mortgage *with no intention of ever using it.*

The closing costs on that decision are high—so why would anyone ever consider that? Simple: to have the option of using it.

If you secure a $500,000 line of credit now, that line of credit is going to grow over time. Imagine that in 20 years, that black swan event occurs, and you need to activate your Katrina Protocols.

That $500,000 line of credit could have grown to $675,000 during that time, which means you have unfettered access to that money—even if the value of your property has collapsed.

The Katrina Protocols are your last line of defense, the strategy you reach for when things have gotten truly dire. The function of establishing your own version of the Katrina Protocols is to know that, even if the worst should happen, you're prepared.

While it's possible you'll never need to invoke your Katrina Protocols, having them in place will increase your feelings of relaxed confidence in retirement.

Conclusions

Filling the Chief Resilience Officer role, whether you do it yourself or outsource your catastrophic thinking to a professional, is one of the most strategic actions you can take when developing your retirement plan. Becoming your own CRO or working with an advisor helps you develop resilience and employ catastrophic thinking *productively*. You should return to your risk planning process every six months or so.

During the time between those six months, you are free to put risk out of your mind and focus on other aspects of your financial plan, which we're going to talk about in the upcoming chapters. Get ready to learn how to ensure you have money in retirement—for life.

Key Takeaways

- **Resilience:** The psychological ability to cope with a crisis or recover from difficulty. The more resilient you are, the quicker you're able to bounce back.

- A Chief Risk Officer's job is to identify and plan for all potential risks; you can act as the CRO of your own retirement plan or outsource that responsibility.

- There are 4 potential responses to risks:

  o **Avoid:** Make a change that eliminates or significantly reduces the odds that a risk comes to pass.

  o **Assume:** Make financial or other preparations for absorbing the cost of an adverse outcome.

  o **Mitigate:** Offset the risk through actions that will offset the impact of an adverse event.

  o **Transfer:** Pay someone else to handle the cost of the risk.

- Risk is always present. Building resilience into your financial plan requires identifying and planning for risks, as well as learning to avoid ruminating.

- Risk management is more than buying an insurance policy.

- There are several major risks to include on your risk register:

  o The stock market might collapse.

  o You might retire into the start of a brutal bear market.

  o Inflation might surge.

  o You might die or become disabled before you retire.

  o You might live to be 100.

    o You might require long-term care.

    o You might get sued.

    o You might experience cognitive decline.

- It's okay to say, "I don't know." You can't know which risk will come to pass, so you need to figure out how to prepare for them all.

- Carrying the largest deductible on your insurance policies allows you to transfer some risks while keeping the total cost of your premiums low.

- Build out your Katrina Protocols—the financial plan you activate if a black swan event occurs.

6. Putting a Floor Beneath Your Feet

Cultivating confidence and optimism, setting goals, and building resilience are foundational parts of your retirement financial plan. Identifying your Needs, Wants, and Wishes provides hints about what your retirement financial plan should look like. In this chapter, we're going to start making that plan concrete.

Your Needs, Wants, and Wishes are great starting points for developing your income floor. An **income floor** is a base salary that you will pay yourself for the rest of your life, using a variety of accounts and portfolios.

Working professionals are accustomed to a base and bonus approach: Your salary arrives in regular intervals throughout the year in the form of a paycheck, and you might get a quarterly or annual bonus based on performance. The base salary of your working life probably covers your Needs and maybe some Wants, while your bonus might fund additional Wants and even some Wishes.

Your retirement income floor is a base salary designed specifically to meet your Needs. Remember from Chapter Four that your Needs are non-negotiable life expenses: housing, food, healthcare, and so on.

An income floor, to get even more specific, is a portion of money that is differentiated from your overall investment portfolio. Its only purpose is to ensure your Needs are met for life.

Let's say you have a portfolio worth $3 million. You might consider sectioning off $1 million to act as an income floor. That money will then be treated exclusively as an income stream for your Needs, rather than as part of your portfolio.

There are many ways to structure your income floor, and we'll explore some options in this chapter. The goal of the income floor is to create a basic level of income that you can rely on no matter what else is going on in the world and in your life.

I'd be hard-pressed to convince most people to take significant investment risks when it comes to meeting their Needs—building an income floor ensures you never have to!

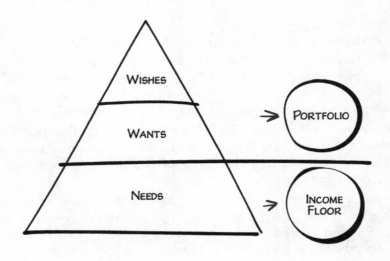

Benefits of Your Income Floor

Creating an income floor as part of your retirement financial plan supports your ability to reach a state of relaxed confidence in retirement. The income floor provides three key benefits— functional, psychological, and behavioral—that support relaxed confidence.

Functional Benefits

The functional benefits of the income floor center on risk mitigation. Establishing an income floor that meets your Needs mitigates interest rate risk, sequence of returns risk, and longevity risk.

Interest rate risk is a risk bond owners face due to fluctuations in interest rates; if interest rates rise, bonds (and other fixed-income investments) decline in value. An income floor insulates you from this type of risk.

Sequence of returns risk represents the danger that there's a market drop in the early years of your retirement which, coupled with withdrawals, exposes you to longevity risk. An income floor protects you from having to make withdrawals during a market downturn just to fund your living expenses.

Longevity risk is the risk of outliving your money. If you build up your income floor with payments you can't outlive, you will be able to fund your non-discretionary expenses.

When you're in the accumulation phase, it doesn't much matter whether any individual year on the market is a good one or a bad one—what matters is the average over the period when you're building wealth. However, when you retire, the sequence of returns becomes much more important.

The most vulnerable period of your investing life is the five years before you retire and the seven to 10 years after. Let's look at an example to see why this period is so critical, and how an income floor can help mitigate sequence of returns risk.

Imagine you retire with a portfolio worth $3 million. That's a great nest egg! However, imagine that in the first two years of your retirement, the stock market takes a significant dip. During that time, your portfolio falls to $1.5 million.

If your plan was to withdraw $100,000 a year from your portfolio to cover your Needs, Wants, and Wishes for the rest of your life, you are suddenly on much shakier ground. Taking $100,000 from a $1.5

million portfolio represents a much larger withdrawal than from a portfolio worth twice that amount.

Part of the problem is that you're no longer contributing to this portfolio during the market slump—in fact, you *must* withdraw from it to cover your basic expenses as well as your Wants and Wishes. Major losses shortly before or after retirement mean your portfolio will struggle to recover.

Even if the average market return across the rest of your life is 10%, your portfolio will lag behind where it was when you started your retirement. It will be challenging for you to live the retirement lifestyle you'd planned on.

Now, let's imagine you retire with a portfolio worth $3 million, and you immediately section off $1 million to act as your income floor, fully covering your Needs. The other $2 million becomes your investment portfolio and is used to fund your Wants and Wishes.

In this scenario, even if the market takes that same dip and your $2 million investment portfolio drops by half to only $1 million, you can still relax comfortably in the knowledge that your Needs are being met by your income floor. No matter what the market does, your basic Needs are covered.

You might scale back some of your Wants and Wishes during the early years of your retirement to give the portfolio a better chance of recovering some lost ground—but you will never have to worry that sequence of returns risk will affect your basic Needs.

The income floor is a great tool for mitigating longevity and sequence of returns risk and makes the case for itself from a practical level.

However, there are also psychological benefits of having an income floor, and these will contribute to your ability to feel a sense of relaxed confidence about your retirement finances.

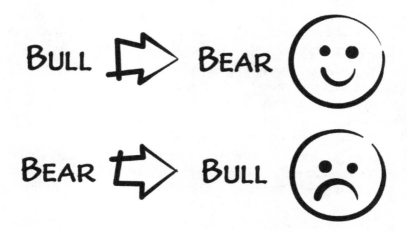

Psychological Benefits

The psychological benefits of establishing an income floor emerge from the knowledge that you have mitigated longevity and sequence of returns risk, and from establishing visibility into your financial planning that will last a lifetime.

Creating an income floor means you will always know that you have a steady "paycheck" coming in to meet your Needs for life. Rather than worrying about having to tap your investment portfolio at the wrong time, you have peace of mind.

One couple comes immediately to mind when I think about the psychological benefits of the income floor. Francis and Susan are 62 years old, and the decade between 62 and 72 turned out to be a crucial one when we sat down to create their financial plan.

There are so many decisions to make when planning your retirement finances, especially during this period. When will you retire? Will you work part-time? When will you take Social Security?

What about Medicare? Will you take a lump sum or regular payments from your employer-sponsored retirement?

Francis and Susan had all these questions and more, and they knew the stakes were high—if there was a major market drop at the start of their retirement, it would be difficult to recover from.

Our challenge was getting them from 62 to 72 with a sense of psychological comfort, a feeling of relaxed confidence. We designed an income floor that would get them from 62 to 70, at which point four additional income streams will kick in: they each have good Social Security benefits, plus a couple of smaller pensions.

As we were looking at their financial plan from 70 on, Francis said, "Well, then we're going to be in Fat City!" Except in this case, Fat City isn't a wild and unattainable goal—it will be their reality!

Not only that, but Francis and Susan are planning to build their dream home before they retire. We were able to add the $1 million in construction costs to their income floor, ensuring the funds they need for their new house aren't subjected to any market risk.

By the time we were done, Francis and Susan had a plan to build their dream home and retire at 64, and they had insight into exactly how they'd fund their lifestyle for the rest of their lives. They left the office with Fat City on the horizon and knew precisely how they'd get there.

That is the psychological benefit of establishing an income floor that's customized to your lifestyle and plans. Once you know your Needs will be met, you also know you don't have to rely on your investment portfolio for income: its only task from then on is to fund your Wants and Wishes.

While you could argue that the idea of the income floor is just an example of mental accounting, the psychological benefit of knowing you have income that will meet your Needs for life cannot be overstated. Building an income floor can move you closer to achieving a feeling of relaxed confidence about your financial life in retirement.

Behavioral Benefits

When you have an income floor in place, you also reap the behavioral benefits—and can allow yourself to enjoy retirement to the fullest.

Building an income floor creates an easy-to-maintain financial plan that will last for the rest of your life. It requires some initial effort to get it set up the way you want it, but once the engine is running, all you need to do is relax and watch the scenery.

An income floor makes it more likely that you will stick to your investment plan. If the market takes a tumble, you won't be among the panicking masses! There's no scramble to protect your assets, no need to fret about the safety of your retirement plan. You already know your Needs are being met. In the worst case scenario, you simply pull back on Wants spending for a time.

The flip side of this behavioral benefit is that an income floor also makes it much easier for you to give yourself permission to enjoy your money in retirement. When you know your Needs are covered, everything else is simply there to be used as you see fit.

Many people struggle with spending when they enter retirement, and it's not hard to see why. After a career spent saving, diligently socking money away, it can be daunting to begin spending it. Without a strong income floor, every little market dip feels like a threat to the stability of your lifestyle.

By sectioning off part of your portfolio specifically to cover your Needs, you free yourself to spend for the fun of it, and to enjoy the retirement you worked so hard to build. If the market performs well, you can treat yourself and your loved ones or make larger donations to charitable organizations without worrying about whether you'll need that money in the future.

An income floor gives you a blueprint for exactly how you'll meet your Needs for the rest of your life—and then gives you permission to go and enjoy the rest of your life with a feeling of relaxed confidence.

Thinking Big About Your Income Floor

Hopefully by now you're sold on the importance of having an income floor, but you might be wondering how to actually build one. It's a bit more complex than simply slicing off a section of your overall retirement nest egg, but the key ingredients are simple!

In this section, we'll review the four most common components of an income floor: Social Security, bond ladders, your pension, and the option of creating a personal pension.

1. Social Security

Social Security is a truly amazing part of your income floor. You cannot outlive this benefit. Social Security is protected from inflation. Social Security is backed up by the federal government.

Your Social Security payments can form a major part of your income floor—and there are ways to optimize the amount of money you'll get.

My biggest piece of advice on Social Security is to defer claiming until age 70. While very few people take advantage of this perk, more people should!

If you're married, consider having one spouse defer until 70 and having the other spouse begin to claim their benefits as part of the income floor. In these cases, the individual with the higher benefit should defer as long as possible, and ideally until 70. If you have the lower benefit, you can consider claiming even before age 66—as young as 62, in some cases!

2. A Ladder

The next component of your income floor is a ladder—a financial instrument that produces money at set intervals (typically three to 10 years).

The most common form is called a bond ladder. Building a bond ladder involves buying and holding bond exchange-traded funds (ETFs) to maturity, with each ETF acting as a "rung." **ETFs** are a type of investment fund built around a particular asset, commodity, index, or sector.

As the bonds mature, the money is distributed to your accounts. Bond ladders are a great way to close gaps between your annual spending and the amount that will be provided through Social Security, a pension, or another retirement account.

Let's say you require $120,000 to meet your Needs each year, and Social Security and your pension account for $90,000 of that amount. This means you have a $30,000 annual gap. That gap can be closed with a bond ladder.

One way to do this is to design a ladder with 10 bond ETFs, or 10 rungs, which you purchase in advance. As each rung matures, it generates the $30,000 you need to round out your income floor.

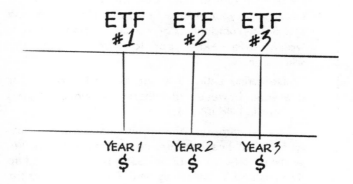

The benefit of this strategy is that a ladder helps insulate you from interest rate risk—something a bond fund can't do.

I recommend using specific year maturing bond ETFs for a bond ladder, rather than individual bonds. ETFs are great for diversifying your portfolio and credit risk.

Let's look at the numbers to make the case for delaying Social Security.

The Social Security Administration says that at age 66, you'll get 100 percent of your monthly benefit.

However, if you delay until age 67, you'll get 108 percent. If you delay until age 70, you get *132 percent* of your monthly benefit! That is a massive increase to your income floor, and if you have the rest of the components of the income floor in place, waiting a few extra years to claim Social Security will be easy.

Deferring until 70 is not the best strategy for everyone, however, and there are nuances based on your individual situation.

For example, many of us underestimate how long we will live, and assume that taking the money earlier is a better financial bet—but if you wind up living past 82, deferring until 70 is absolutely the better outcome.

NERDING OUT!

Using specific year maturing bond ETFs creates an even surer bet for the stability of your income floor. Invesco and iShares have amazing low-cost specific year maturing investment-grade corporate ETFs that include hundreds of bonds and are a great option.

The second type of ladder is called a **MYGA**, or a multi-year guaranteed annuity. Some people, whose conviction around their spending needs and financial strategy is extremely high, use a MYGA instead of the more common bond ladder.

A MYGA has all the same functional benefits of a bond ladder, with a few key differences. Instead of purchasing ETFs, you purchase a guaranteed annuity from an insurance company. A MYGA typically has a higher rate of return than a bond fund, which is great for increasing the amount of money you'll have access to.

The downside to a MYGA is that it's not liquid. If you purchase a MYGA and change your mind, there is a substantial penalty you must pay to access that money again. It's for this reason that I only recommend a MYGA if you are certain it's the right strategy for you. If you think you might change your mind, stick with a traditional bond ladder.

Whatever method you choose, there are two ways to think about your ladder. One is as a bridge to Social Security. Let's say you retire at age 62 and plan on deferring Social Security until age 70.

You can build an 8-year ladder that gets you from 62 to 70, and then let Social Security take over! This option works best if Social Security and your pension will cover your Needs, or at least most of them.

The second option is to think about a ladder as a long-term strategy. If you don't have much in the way of a pension, you may want to extend your ladder past 70, perhaps to 80 or even longer.

If this is the case, you'll need to replenish your ladder—you can think of it as adding rungs to the ladder—using your investment portfolio.

Adding a rung to your ladder is simple enough. Once a year, when you rebalance your portfolio, you will simply sell enough stocks and/or bonds to purchase another rung.

Imagine that you built a ladder with $100,000 per rung to get you to age 70, when Social Security kicks in. If your Social Security benefit is $40,000, then each rung of your ladder after that only needs to be $60,000 to allow you to maintain the same level of spending. If your combined (you plus your spouse) Social Security benefit is $70,000, then each rung of your ladder after that only needs to be $30,000.

Imagine you're maintaining an eight-year ladder, and it costs $50,000 today to buy shares of an ETF that will mature for $60,000 in eight years. When you rebalance your portfolio, you remove $50,000 and purchase the required number of shares of the specific-year maturity in your dedicated ladder account.

A ladder is a great option for creating an income floor, especially if you don't have a robust pension plan. Fortunately, there are also options for creating your own personal pension, which can also be used to form part of your income floor.

3. A Company Pension

Although pensions have largely gone by the wayside, some employers still provide them. According to the AARP, more than half of Americans report that having a pension would increase their confidence in retirement, and more than eight in 10 Americans are worried about their ability to retire.[42]

The decrease in pensions and the rise of individual plans like 401(k)s account for a lot of this anxiety. If you are lucky enough to have a pension, you are in awesome shape. If you don't have an employer-sponsored pension, skip to the next section to find out how you can create your own.

A pension is another wonderful part of an income floor, because pension plans ensure you have an additional monthly source of income that you cannot outlive. Pensions also sometimes provide

---

[42] AARP NRTA (n.d.)

other benefits, like disability protections; if you have a pension, be sure to examine it carefully to see everything the plan offers. [43]

If you have a choice between taking a lump sum and signing up for monthly payments, I encourage you to take the monthly payments. The rate of return on taking these payments seems low, and it is tempting to want to take the lump sum up front and invest it. Many advisors will actually advise you to take the lump sum so they can manage it (and profit off of it themselves), a conflict of interest we'll talk about further in Chapter Thirteen.

However, the beauty of the payments is that they'll never run out and they make your income floor robust and predictable. If you build an income floor, you won't need to take the lump sum and put it into stocks to fund your Needs, Wants, and Wishes—you'll already have an investment portfolio for that!

One client of mine, for example, has worked with me on designing an income floor and portfolio that meet her Needs, Wants, and Wishes. In fact, she has the most robust income floor imaginable—at 73, she has a generous pension from the government that includes built-in cost of living adjustments. This inflation-protected pension covers her Needs and a decent amount of her Wants.

Because of this, she has a portfolio that is 100% stocks. Most financial advisors, given her age, would insist on a 60/40 stock/bond split. Since all her Needs are met by her pension, she's able to weather a significant amount of risk to invest and reap the rewards in the form of funding travel, preparing to leave money to her heirs, and supporting charities.

If you have a pension that is big enough to support your Needs (and maybe a little extra), you can afford to take on additional risks. You can think of this as a return to the base/bonus framework: The pension now acts as your base salary, covering your Needs and some of your Wants. In years when the market performs well, you can pay yourself larger bonuses to fund additional Wants and Wishes; if the

---

[43] Ibid.

stock market falls a bit, you can sleep easy, knowing that your Needs are covered.

4. A Personal Pension

You might not know this already, but there is a way for you to buy a pension on the open market. If you already have a generous company pension, this strategy is overkill.

However, if you are someone who has a small pension or no pension at all, this is an idea to consider! What you would actually be buying is an income annuity.

Now, don't let the word annuity scare you off! I understand the aversion to annuities. They're expensive, they're complex, they're confusing, and they're oversold. Salespeople tend to push annuities hard because of the commission they'll get. People are wary of annuities for good reason!

However, there have been innovations that make certain types of annuities attractive when you think of them as creating a do-it-yourself pension. The "commission-free annuity" can make a world of difference for people without a significant company pension. Stripping out the commission allows the insurance company to make several terms of the annuity contract more favorable to the buyer.

You can think of a commission-free annuity as a type of bond ladder that has the bonus of being packaged with a form of longevity insurance. Only an insurance company can offer you that combination! An income annuity is a bond ladder that you can never outlive, making this a great addition to your income floor.

INCOME ANNUITY = BOND LADDER + LONGEVITY INSURANCE

One person to follow on this topic is retirement researcher Dr. Wade Pfau, who runs the Retirement Income Certified Professional course. He argues in favor of considering annuities as part of an overall retirement strategy.[44]

There are two types of commission-free annuities you should consider for your retirement: the pure income annuity and the fixed income annuity.

Single Premium Immediate Annuity (SPIA)

The pure income annuity is a Single Premium Immediate Annuity (SPIA). "Single Premium" is the check you'll write up front, and "Immediate Annuity" means you'll start collecting your payments immediately.

The way it works is actually quite simple: You exchange an asset for an income stream. That is, you write a big check to an insurance company in exchange for a promise—in the form of a contract—that the insurance company will pay you a certain amount of money every month, for the rest of your life.

For example, at the time of this writing, you could write a $1 million check to an insurance company, which is then going to turn around and pay you $5,000 a month, forever. This is the purest form of longevity insurance you can get.

You can also defer the start of the payments to increase them. Say you're considering purchasing an SPIA at age 60. Instead, you could write a much smaller check to the company, in exchange for a contract that states they'll start paying you that income for life when you turn 80. This becomes an affordable way to transfer your longevity risk to an insurance company—think of it as a deferred income annuity.

You win the bet with the insurance company if you live into your

---

[44] Pechter, K. (2019).

90s. The drawback is that you lose the bet if you die early. If you were to get hit by a bus the day after you sign the SPIA contract, that money is gone.

Fixed Income Annuity (FIA)

The second option allows you to have your cake and eat it too. Loss aversion and aversion to annuities lead many people to prefer the second option, the Fixed Income Annuity (FIA). If you want your cake (income for life) and to eat it too (the ability to change your mind and get your money back), you should consider an FIA with an Income Rider, also called a Living Benefit Rider, which means the insurance company promises to pay you a certain amount of money—for life.

What makes this different from a bond mutual fund is the Income Rider, which ensures you will be paid a certain amount of money for life—even if your account value drops to $0. The rider costs about 1% per year.

As with the SPIA, you can defer the start date of the payments. In the case of the FIA, let's say you signed the contract for $1 million at age 60 and decide to start collecting income at age 70, when the account has grown to $1.2 million. You'll receive $5,000 each month for the rest of your life.

If you die at 80 and there's $300,000 left in the account value, that money can go to your heirs. If you live to 87, the account value will be depleted—but you will keep receiving $5,000 checks each month until you die!

The other benefit of the FIA is that you can get your money back. Let's say you purchase an FIA for $1 million but, for whatever reason, change your mind. If you unwind the annuity within the first five years, you'll have to pay a surrender charge—but you can reclaim those funds!

The Fixed Indexed Annuity (FIA) has a few moving parts. Let's say you purchase an FIA for $1 million. The insurance company invests the $1 million, and you'll have an account with the company that's worth $1 million.

Rather than getting a set amount of money each month, your return from the FIA will vary each year between a set floor and ceiling. The floor is a return of 0%, meaning you didn't lose money, but not much else. At the time of this writing, the actual return tends to be between 0% and 8%, which will be driven by the index associated with the FIA.

Despite this more complicated formula, you can think of the FIA as a bond substitute: you'll be invested in bonds and will receive bond-like returns.

NERDING OUT!

Most annuities are sold on a commission basis, and those commissions can be large. This results in aggressive salespeople pushing products that aren't actually in their clients' best interests. It also results in a reduction of your returns, thanks to those significant commissions.

The benefit of both the SPIA and FIA is that there are commission-free versions you can seek out. The rise of the commission-free annuity strips out the commission expense, resulting in more favorable terms for you. Both income annuities can be used as a substitute for a company pension and can help fund a significant portion of your income floor.

Conclusions

Imagine the sense of relaxed confidence that emerges from knowing your Needs are going to be met for life—no matter what happens, your basic expenses are going to be covered. You cannot outlive your money. Sequence of returns risk cannot put you out of house and home. Empowering, isn't it?

However, there's more to life than just meeting your basic Needs. You also have Wants and Wishes to account for—and that's where the perfect portfolio comes in. We'll look at investing in the next couple of chapters and explore how to design a portfolio that provides for your Wants and Wishes as well.

Key Takeaways

- **Income floor:** A salary you will pay yourself for the rest of your life that ensures all your Needs are met.

- An income floor mitigates longevity risk and sequence of returns risk by covering all your Needs.
  - **Longevity risk:** The risk that you will outlive your money.

- o **Sequence of returns risk:** The risk that a market drop in the early years of your retirement exposes you to longevity risk.

- The most vulnerable period of your investing life is the five years before and the seven to 10 years after you retire.

- An income floor increases feelings of relaxed confidence by mitigating risk and establishing lifelong visibility into your financial plan.

- There are four common components of an income floor:
  - o Social Security. Social Security payments are especially valuable if you defer until age 70.
  - o A ladder. Bond and MYGA ladders can help fill in any gaps between your Social Security income and annual Needs.
  - o A pension. The monthly payment option from a company pension provides stable, predictable income.
  - o A personal pension. Purchasing a commission-free income annuity allows you to create your own personal pension.

7. The Greatest Game?

We didn't have classes on Wednesdays when I was in business school at Stanford so, naturally, my buddies and I would head to Vegas on Tuesday afternoons. We'd sit at the blackjack table for hours.

Blackjack is a game that requires both luck and skill, which was what attracted us to it. We'd try to memorize all the statistically optimal plays, and a few of us learned to count cards (although we were too distracted by the free drinks to get really good. One woman in my class at Harvard made a killing on a blackjack team that became the subject of both a book and a movie, but that's another story!).

Those blackjack sessions were epic, but we had the most fun at the craps table. There's an amazing amount of camaraderie at the craps table. You can easily have 15 people cheering for you each time you throw the dice.

Unlike blackjack, craps is a game of pure chance, although you'd never know it based on how some people approach it. I've seen folks blow on the dice before they'll roll, always use the same hand to throw the dice, release the dice at a specific angle, say the same lucky phrase before each toss—you name it.

In contrast to blackjack, though, craps players don't have any real control over the outcome. You can't learn to control the randomness of a dice roll. Yet people try to exert some form of control through the rituals they perform before each toss, even though we know, rationally, that the result comes down to chance.

We've already discussed how to build an income floor that will meet your Needs for life. In this chapter, we're going to start talking about the games of investing, and specifically the game of stock picking. Playing the wrong game can be costly.

Games of Chance & Skill

I've played hundreds of games of all varieties. I enjoy some a great deal, and some not so much. I've done a lot of thinking about games, and I think one critical dimension that people miss is identifying where a game falls on the Chance-Skill Continuum.

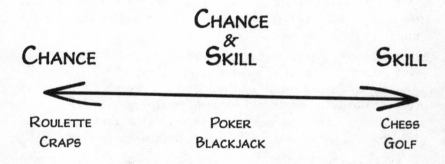

Understanding the nature of the game you're playing is of paramount importance. You can obviously have fun playing games of chance and games of skill and everything in between—but when it comes to investing, the nature of the game becomes serious indeed.

The 3 Investing Games

All games come down to a few simple elements: your goals, how you play, the costs, the risks, and the nature of the game. Let's look at each type of investing game.

There are three basic investing games. These games are different from one another. You also need to choose one type of investing game to focus on—at least for now; we'll discuss how to play more than one game in the following chapters.

When it comes to investing, the three basic games are Stock Picking, Portfolio Management, and Wealth Management.

- Stock Picking is mostly a game of chance. It is based largely on luck.

- Portfolio Management falls in the middle, with a mix of chance and skill.

- Wealth Management is a game of skill, requiring expertise and knowledge.

For the purposes of this chapter, your goal is to learn about the stock picking game, where it falls on the chance/skill continuum and why, and to decide whether this is the game you really want to play. In Chapter Eight, we'll look at the other two investing games you have to choose from.

Game #1: Picking Stocks

Unless you follow mutual fund managers closely, it's likely you haven't heard the story I'm about to tell you.

Not that long ago, there was an extremely successful fund manager whose name is irrelevant for our purposes. He oversaw the flagship mutual fund for a major managed investment and asset management firm. Not only did he manage a large fund, but this man also went on quite a run between the years 1992 and 2004—in that he beat the market every year during that period.

He was the *only* fund manager to do so.

Let me show you more clearly what he did:

- **1992: He beat the market**
- **1993: He beat the market**
- **1994: He beat the market**
- **1995: He beat the market**

- **1996: He beat the market**
- **1997: He beat the market**
- **1998: He beat the market**
- **1999: He beat the market**
- **2000: He beat the market**
- **2001: He beat the market**
- **2002: He beat the market**
- **2003: He beat the market**
- **2004: He beat the market**

That sure looks like a pattern to me. Would you agree?

I've spent my share of time in casinos, and I've never seen someone successfully choose whether the ball would land on red or black *13 times in a row*. Beating a 50% chance of success that many times is nearly unheard of.

So, the performance here certainly looks like skill—and it seems like it blows a pretty big hole in the argument that stock picking is largely a game of chance. However, before I admit defeat on this point, we need to take a step back and look at the bigger picture.

Let's look at this success another way.

There were about 8,000 mutual funds in the U.S. during the period when this fund manager repeatedly beat the S&P 500.

Now, I used to live in San Francisco, and I enjoyed visiting the Bill Graham Civic Center, which can hold 8,500 people. Imagine we've hopped in a time machine and invited all 8,000 or so mutual fund managers to the Bill Graham Civic Center in 1991.

Let's give each one of them a quarter and ask them to keep flipping that quarter until it comes up tails. Once a fund manager flips tails, they must sit down, put the quarter in their pocket, and wait.

Simple statistics tell us how this game will unfold:

- After nine flips, there are only nine mutual fund managers still flipping quarters.

- After 11 flips, we're down to four fund managers on their feet.

- After 13 flips, there is just one guy still flipping a quarter: our flagship fund manager!

His prize for this little game was $70 billion of assets under management, which generated more than $700 million per year in fees for him and his team, because so many people were—understandably—captivated by the fact that he kept flipping heads.

The math tells us that to produce one person who flips 13 heads in a row, you need to start with around 8,000 people flipping quarters. That is remarkably close to the number of mutual funds in existence during this unprecedented run.

It's not necessarily that this fund manager had any special skills, insight, or knowledge. He was simply the statistically inevitable lucky person who flipped heads 13 times in a row.

You might be wondering what happened after his streak ended. What happened was that the fund fell off a cliff. Ultimately, only about $20 billion of the original $70 billion was salvaged from the wreckage.

One more thing to think about: if you believe you could wander into the Bill Graham Civic Center, look at the group of folks in nearly identical suits and pick out the person who'll get 13 heads in a row before he does—and then predict how long his lucky streak will last once it's started—we should talk. I've got some amazing investment ideas for you!

The safest assumption to make is that stock picking is a game of chance that *looks* like a game of skill, in large part thanks to significant outliers.

The Goal of Stock Picking

The goal of picking stocks is simple: You want to beat the market!

Stock picking offers the promise of quick earnings, especially if you're able to identify a hot stock, get in early, and time your exit correctly. The goal is to be just enough faster than everyone else playing that you're able to walk away with major profits.

How You Play the Stock Picking Game

There are several ways to play the stock picking game.

You can play the stock picking game using your own intuition. Maybe you have a good gut feeling about the latest innovative tech company. Maybe you simply feel like a particular stock is about to skyrocket.

You can play based on a story someone told you. Maybe you follow the daily stock ticker or have a favorite financial analyst who's really been pushing a particular purchase in recent weeks.

You can conduct fundamental analysis and crunch all the numbers—profit margins, growth, etc.—and analyze industry structure and competitive dynamics.

You can use technical analysis, which will have you staring at charts of stock price movements until you find (or imagine) a pattern you think you can exploit.

You can get on Reddit. You can throw darts. You can ask your grandchild what they think.

The Cost of Playing at Picking Stocks

The cost of the stock picking game is layered. There are initial costs, and there are the hidden costs.

One cost comes from picking stocks yourself. While it's become inexpensive to buy and sell individual stocks, the process is not totally free. While many platforms don't charge for trading commissions, you must factor in spreads (the difference between what you can buy a stock for and what you can sell it for) and taxes.

Still, though, you can buy and hold—or buy and trade—quite a lot of stocks relatively inexpensively.

You can also pay for advice. While you can generate your own ideas or get advice from friends or much of the financial media for free, you can also pay to subscribe to stock-picking newsletters. They'll charge you $200 a year for their basic stock advising service, and then try to upsell you to a $5,000 per year "boss mode" premium service.

You could also delegate your stock picking to a paid professional, who will charge you a percentage fee for the privilege. Let's say you have a $2 million portfolio, and you ask a professional stock picker to manage it for you. They'll likely charge you a 1% fee, or $20,000 per year.

If your stock picker is buying individual stocks themselves, you're only in for the $20,000. However, if your stock picker turns around and subcontracts four additional specialized stock pickers—for different sectors and strategies, for example—that $20,000 could quickly double to $40,000 per year.

The cost of all of this adds up, and it takes a huge bite out of your overall portfolio. Even if you only hire a professional stock picker who does not hire subcontractors, a 1% fee creates significant head wind for the growth of your portfolio.

Let me explain this cost another way.

We'll assume, for the purposes of this illustration, that you invested $2 million with an individual stock picker who manages to deliver market performance across a 25-year period. Your $2 million investment will grow to $6.8 million over that period, assuming 1% fees and 5% annual returns. That doesn't sound too bad, at first glance!

But now let's imagine that, instead, you chose to simply stick your $2 million in a low-cost ETF account with a company like Vanguard or Blackrock. Across that same 25-year period, your investment would have grown to *$8.6 million*—simply because the fees are so low that you basically get the full 6% average return.

The stock picker's fees alone ate $1.2 million that could have been yours to spend on your Wants and Wishes.

Overall, passive investing beats active investing by a significant margin.

Now, of course, actual performance with a professional stock picker won't look exactly like this—they might outperform the market, or they could do much worse. Either way, the individual stock picker is all but guaranteed to have to climb out of a $1.8 million hole, minimum, just because of their fees!

One of my clients, Donna, lost her husband a few years before we started working together. Donna's husband had managed the finances before his death, and for another decade, Donna kept things pretty much as they were. She worked with a traditional wealth advisor who charged her a 1% fee and had her invested in some extremely expensive mutual funds and 300 individual stocks.

Her $4 million portfolio cost $40,000 a year for the advisor alone, plus another $20,000 for the mutual funds. Donna felt trapped by the complexity of the whole portfolio: there was no way she wanted to manage all those positions.

Then, Donna attended a workshop and a financial coach recommended she reach out to me. After a series of conversations, Donna recognized the $60,000+ annual cost and unnecessary complexity represented a major drag on both her portfolio and her peace of mind. Think about that $60,000 a year multiplied by the 10 years since her husband had died!

As we discussed her options, Donna had a eureka moment. After assuming for her entire adult life that wealth managers knew a bunch of things she didn't (thus justifying the huge price tag), she saw a path to significantly reduce her expenses, improve diversification, enhance her tax efficiency, and streamline her portfolio, making it easier to understand and manage.

It was as if the weight of the world lifted off her shoulders. Donna, who is charitably inclined, redirected a significant portion of the money she saved into a donor-advised fund that allows her to give each year.

Now that she's invested in low-cost ETFs, Donna also has insight into her portfolio, feels more confident about managing it, and doesn't have to struggle uphill against those management and mutual fund expenses.

As Donna is discovering, putting money into an ETF and leaving it alone means you'll get results that beat most professional stock pickers in the long run—and it doesn't create the same drag traditional wealth management does.

Ask yourself: is stock picking a game you really want to be playing? Is the price tag worth it?

The Risk of Stock Picking

The risk of stock picking isn't only that the costs can be astronomical. The biggest risk is that you end up unable to fund your Wants and Wishes, thanks to an unlucky portfolio.

There are plenty of professional investors who will claim that all you need is a selection of 15 to 30 stocks to enjoy the benefits of

Research has shown that a small number of super-stocks (Amazon, Apple) drive most of the gains of the stock market. Researcher Ron Surz ran a fascinating analysis on this topic: He created 1,000 portfolios with 15 randomly chosen stocks in each, and he tested what happened over 30 years.[*]

The lucky portfolios in Surz's analysis (those in the 95th percentile) ended with 2.5 times the portfolio invested in the market. The unlucky portfolios (those in the 5th percentile)? They ended up being worth 60% less than the portfolio invested in the market!

That is a massive difference—and there is no way to know ahead of time which stocks will turn out to be lucky, and which will not.

[*] Bernstein, W.J. (2009)

NERDING OUT!

diversification. While 15-30 stocks will reduce the expected deviation of returns for the portfolio, what does the advice truly produce?

Not much, as it turns out! What these pros miss is the difference between lucky and unlucky portfolios, especially with such a small number of stocks in the mix.

The Nature of the Stock Picking Game

I have concluded through long experience and study that stock picking is mostly a game of luck. Part of the issue is that when we see someone who's succeeded at stock picking, especially over a long period of time, our brains are predisposed to see that result as a pattern emerging from skill.

In truth, though, it's more often the illusion of skill combined with several other factors unrelated to securities selection.

The game of stock picking can be thrilling and exhilarating. During my time peddling investment advice at the Motley Fool, we constantly talked about the "10 Baggers," or the picks we made that then increased 10 times in value. It was a rush! But were these 10 Baggers the result of skill or luck?

The evidence suggests it was luck. University of Chicago Economics Professor and Nobel Prize Winner Eugene Fama has studied the stock market for decades, and his research in the *Financial Analysts Journal* suggests stock pickers simply cannot consistently beat the market—the outliers are simply that: outliers who have managed to get very, very lucky.[45]

Larry Swedroe, chief research officer for Buckingham Wealth Partners and co-author of *The Incredible Shrinking Alpha*, shared in an interview that stock picking doesn't work in part because it's based on the misplaced belief that the market is underpricing stocks.[46]

In fact, the market is increasingly efficient at pricing stocks

---

[45] Fama, E. F. (1965).
[46] Pisani, B. (2020).

correctly—which means simply investing in an index fund that mimics the overall market will consistently deliver better and more accurate returns than paying someone to try to outsmart the market.

Even I will admit that, yes, there are some people who manage to beat the market (although I'd still argue that it's mainly luck). However, the evidence is clear that there is no way to identify a priori who actually has that skill and can deliver results that will beat the market *and* beat the benefits of simply investing in a low-cost index fund.

It's typically going to take until the end of a full market cycle to identify such a person, and by then the asset bloat that comes with success can dampen their skill. Do you really want to wait 10 years and bet $1 million or more that you could otherwise spend on your Wants and Wishes that you found the proverbial needle in a haystack?

The evidence repeatedly suggests that stock picking, like craps, is a game of chance.

What About Warren?

Now I know that many of you reading this chapter have had one question in mind: *What about Warren?*

Warren Buffett is the single most successful investor the world has ever seen. Over his many decades of investing, he's amassed a net worth of $125 billion. That is a staggering amount of money. Not only that, but Berkshire Hathaway has outperformed all other U.S. mutual funds that have existed for similar lengths of time.[47]

How can I possibly account for the existence of Warren Buffett and still argue that stock picking is mostly based on luck?

Let me show you.

As I said earlier in the chapter, we're predisposed to look for and

---

[47] Frazzini, A., Kabiller, D., and Pedersen, L. H. (2019).

see patterns—even when we might be wrong. Warren Buffett's story is a great example of this. Many people simply don't understand or aren't aware of the role played by factors outside of stock selection in building wealth, and yet there's evidence to suggest that those factors have played an enormous role in Buffett's success.

First, Buffett has been investing for over 70 years. He started investing when he was a teenager, and he's now in his 90s. Seventy plus years is more than enough time to build a tremendous amount of wealth, even if you just put that money into an index fund.

This factor alone is not enough to explain Buffett's track record of *beating* the market, of course, but even if you put $100,000 into a black box and let it grow for 70 years, you're still going to wind up with a substantial fortune. Buffett is quite an old man, and he started investing much earlier in life than many of the rest of us.

Second, Buffett has displayed unwavering fortitude throughout his entire investing career. What I mean by that is that he decided to invest in stocks—and then didn't blink, for more than 70 years.

Most investors blink. When things get scary, people make bad decisions: they try to time the market, sell at inopportune moments and buy at worse ones, and generally behave in irrational ways. Buffett decided on his course over 70 years ago and has never wavered.

Third, Buffett has engaged in massive borrowing. Buffett has been invested 160% or more in stocks and 0% in bonds. How do you get to be 160% in stocks, like Buffett did, when the average investor is maybe 60% in stocks and 40% in bonds? Debt. Extraordinary amounts of debt.

If you have, say, $1 billion invested in stocks, banks are going to allow you to borrow another $600 million—you've got $1 billion in collateral, after all! Buffett was able to leverage a massive amount of debt, and that one strategy winds up explaining a substantial amount of his ability to outperform the market. If you borrowed $600 million at 3% and earned 10% on $1.6 billion, you'd be sitting pretty too. However, this is a wildly risky strategy, and not something I would ever recommend.

Finally, Buffett's portfolio is tilted towards value stocks, a strategy called value investing. We'll talk more about this strategy in Chapter Eight. There was certainly an element of skill in Buffett's selection of a value strategy—but selecting a value strategy is not the same as making good decisions about individual securities.

Not only was Buffett investing during some of the most impressive bull runs ever seen, but value stocks also outperformed the rest of the market during most of that time. As with leverage, the value strategy helps explain even more of Buffett's investing success.

Let's pull all of this together: Buffett

- has had a longer-than-average investing career,

- possesses a backbone of steel,

- engaged in astronomical levels of borrowing, and

- tilted his portfolio towards a type of stock that happened to outperform the rest of the market.

Those factors together explain the vast majority of Buffett's current net worth.

Those factors, however, still don't account for *all* of Buffett's wealth. I will admit that some percentage of Buffett's success might be attributed to skill. However, I'll argue (as do many financial analysts and scholars), given the factors above, that skill accounts for only a tiny percentage of Buffett's total net worth.

As statistician and author Nassim Taleb put it, "I am not saying Buffett doesn't have skill—I'm just saying we don't have enough evidence to say Buffett isn't doing it by chance."[48] The sample size is simply too small to make a firm declaration one way or the other.

---

[48] PR Newswire. (2010).

A net worth of $125 billion, on its face, seems like it can only be explained by extraordinary skill at stock picking. It's only when you start to examine the whole of Buffett's strategy, factor by factor, that you start to see how elements other than stock selection account for his results.

So here are the questions we're really left with: Given Warren Buffett's existence and results, is it fair to argue that skill exists in stock picking today? Let's say yes—to a degree.

If we assume skill exists, can you identify a person with skill a priori—that is, *before* they have started to produce results? That's extremely unlikely. How will you find them? Are they writing a blog? Tweeting? Shouting their stock picks on the street?

And even if you could identify a person with stock picking skill a priori, look again at Warren Buffett's results: The vast majority of his wealth comes from factors unrelated to stock selection itself.

What's to say a person who's skilled at picking stocks also has the right strategy, or a firm enough constitution to stay the course when everyone else is panicking?

Stock picking skill, if it exists, is too risky and has too small an impact to base your entire investment strategy around it. Still not convinced? Let's hear from the man himself.

In an annual Berkshire Hathaway meeting, Warren Buffett said, "I do not think the average person can pick stocks."[49] Instead, he suggests the everyday investor put their money into low-cost index funds, and that he has recommended the S&P 500 "for a long, long time."[50]

Not only that, but most of Buffett's own money will be invested in the S&P 500 upon his death. As Buffett put it, "I just think that the best thing to do is buy 90% in S&P 500 index fund."[51]

---

[49] Locke, T. (2021).
[50] Ibid.
[51] Ibid.

Conclusions

When it comes to your investment portfolio, you can take a chance and play the stock picking game, attempting to beat the market while taking on the highest level of risk when it comes to being able to fund your Wants and Wishes.

Stock picking looks like a game of skill—but the truth is that it's most often a game of chance, and even the most successful investor of all time thinks it's not the right game to play. In the next chapter, we'll move a little closer to the skill end of the continuum and look at the next two games you can play: portfolio management and wealth management.

Key Takeaways

- All games fall somewhere on a continuum between chance and skill. Craps is a game of chance; chess is a game of skill.

- Understanding the nature of the game you're playing is important—and it's essential when that game is investing.

- There are three types of investing games you can play:
    - Stock Picking: A game of chance.
    - Portfolio Management: A game of chance and skill.
    - Wealth Management: A game of skill.

- There are always outliers in stock picking who manage to make it seem like a game of skill—don't be fooled!

- It is impossible to identify a lucky stock picker a priori, or to predict how long their luck will last.

- The game of stock picking costs time and money in the form of taxes, advice, and stock pickers' fees. You could also lose your entire portfolio if you get unlucky!

- A 1% stock picker fee might sound low, but it creates significant drag on the total value of your portfolio. A low-cost index fund will almost always beat active stock picking.

- Research repeatedly shows that stock pickers cannot consistently beat the market.

8. Managing Your Portfolio vs. Your Wealth

Playing the stock picking game is one that some people see as the best and fastest path to retirement wealth. However, as we saw in the last chapter, stock picking is mostly a game of chance—and the most skilled investor the world has ever seen suggests the average investor shouldn't even try to play it.

Fortunately, as we move along the chance-skill continuum, there are other options to consider. In this chapter, you'll learn about the two remaining investing games: portfolio management, a game that blends luck and skill, and wealth management—in my opinion, the investing game that combines the highest amount of skill, the lowest amount of risk, and the best odds of success.

Let's dive in.

Game #2: Portfolio Management

During my time at Stanford, one course changed how I saw the world of investing forever. The class was called Modern Portfolio Theory, and it was taught by Nobel Laureate Bill Sharpe.

Professor Sharpe shared the arithmetic of active investing with those of us taking the course. I illustrated some of that content in Chapter Seven as part of my description of the difference between active and passive portfolios, and the massive difference between hiring a stock picker and putting your money into a low-cost ETF.

Sharpe helped us shift our focus from analyzing individual stocks to understanding the characteristics of an entire portfolio, instead. This represented a huge mental shift for those of us in the class, and it's at the core of what it means to play the investing game of portfolio management.

The Goal of Portfolio Management

The aim of portfolio management is maximizing expected returns for your entire portfolio, for any given level of expected risk. Given that goal, the characteristics of any individual security are, in fact, irrelevant.

This concept blew my mind. It was a true eureka moment!

One of my favorite things is helping my clients reach that eureka moment themselves. Take the Smiths: Paul and Nancy had a standard array of investment accounts, including some 401(k)s, IRAs, taxable investments, and an inheritance.

When we first worked together, Paul and Nancy were extremely focused on the individual account and security level. They'd ask me what I suggested they do with specific accounts and asset allocations—common questions, since most people experience their money at the account or security level.

Think of any individual security as a tree. If you get too focused on the trees, you miss seeing the forest. That's what the Smiths were experiencing.

Through our time working together, I helped Paul and Nancy take a step back and refocus their attention at the level of the forest, or their entire portfolio. Portfolio theory shows us that it's the characteristics of the portfolio as a whole that matter—not the characteristics of any one security.

By refocusing Paul and Nancy's attention at the level of their $5 million portfolio instead of individual accounts within it, we were able to reduce the complexity significantly by asking a simple question: How much of the portfolio should be in safe assets, and how much should be in speculative assets?

That was the eureka moment for Paul and Nancy. Rather than getting concerned that a particular bond yield in a specific account seemed low, or worrying about how to allocate funds in a particular account, they could take a step back: was their portfolio *as a whole* balanced the way they wanted between safety and risk? Would the balance maximize returns while minimizing risks? If yes, then they were set!

Modern portfolio theory can help you achieve a sense of relaxed confidence by helping you focus on the forest, not the trees. Through his research on modern portfolio theory, Sharpe gave the world a useful tool which came to be known, appropriately enough, as the Sharpe Ratio.[52]

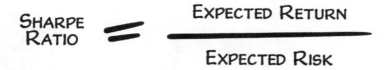

$$\text{SHARPE RATIO} = \frac{\text{EXPECTED RETURN}}{\text{EXPECTED RISK}}$$

The brilliance of the Sharpe Ratio lies in its simplicity. The ratio measures a portfolio's expected return for each unit of risk the portfolio faces.

Any good investment manager should be attempting to maximize this ratio. The ratio can be maximized by, for example, adding or subtracting securities to increase the numerator or decrease the denominator.

How You Play the Portfolio Management Game

A bunch of geeks with lots of powerful computers decided to crunch a lot of data—and you can benefit from that data easily enough.

In fact, if you want a portfolio with an outstanding Sharpe Ratio, here's all you need to do: Buy a small slice of the total global stock market.

---

[52] Sharpe, W. F. (1994).

That's it!

Vanguard, BlackRock, and other companies that offer ETFs are incredibly popular options for this approach, in part because they are so inexpensive. The low expense ratios are why Vanguard, in particular, had surpassed $7 trillion under management as of 2021— yes, that's trillion with a T.

Vanguard's founder, Jack Bogle, has a number of excellent quotations. My personal favorite is, "In investing, you get what you *don't* pay for."[53]

In other words, if you keep the money that would have gone to the stock picker, the positive impact on your portfolio across time is likely to be profound.

Two researchers from the University of Chicago, Eugene Fama and Kenneth French, proposed a twist on the "own all the stocks" approach. In their work, Fama and French found a couple of anomalies that have persisted over the last 70 years, and across stock markets around the world.[54]

What Fama and French discovered is that small cap stocks (or stocks of smaller companies) and value stocks (stocks with a low ratio of market value to book value) both tend to outperform the overall market. Value investing is the strategy Warren Buffett used, as we discussed in Chapter Seven.

An entire company, called Dimensional Fund Advisors (DFA) was founded on top of the Fama-French research, and it's become an incredibly successful organization. Choosing DFA over a company like Vanguard costs a bit more, although the expense ratio is still low. You also still technically own all the stocks—the only difference is that your portfolio is slightly tiled toward small and value stocks.

[53] Bogle, J. C. (2005).
[54] Fama, E. F. and French, K. R. (1996).

The Cost of Portfolio Management

If you decide to be your own portfolio manager and use a company like BlackRock or Vanguard, you can own all the stocks for as low as five basis points—or 1/20th of 1%. If you have $2 million in an account with that expense ratio, your annual cost would only be $1,000.

That is a truly amazing outcome, especially compared to the astronomical cost and risk associated with hiring a stock picker.

If you decide to outsource the effort and hire someone to manage your portfolio for you, things start to get interesting...

Let's imagine you buy into the factor investing option, and decide you want to purchase your funds from DFA. Currently, these funds are only available through investment advisors—although DFA has started to release ETFs for everyone. A DFA portfolio will run you about 0.20%, or $4,000 per year on a $2 million portfolio.

However, you also have the cost of the advisor, which runs you about another $20,000 each year. Many professional investment managers understandably feel the need to justify that $20,000 price tag—so what do they do?

Unfortunately, far too many of them undo the incredible results of the low-cost ETF and try to beat the market by sub-contracting to professional stock pickers! Choosing a portfolio manager can be just as expensive, if not more so, than working with an individual stock picker.

NERDING OUT!

The Risk of Portfolio Management

The risks associated with portfolio management aren't as severe as the risks associated with stock picking—but that doesn't mean you're off the hook entirely. Portfolio management still has a few key risks you need to consider.

First, there's the risk of insufficient diversification. If your portfolio lacks appropriate amounts of diversification across asset classes, asset allocation, and asset location (a concept we'll talk about further in Chapter Ten), you run the risk of watching your portfolio fluctuate sharply due to market gyrations or a downturn in a specific industry.

Second, you need to consider tax drag. Tax drag encompasses the losses you experience in your returns because of the taxes you wind up paying on investments that aren't tax-sheltered. While tax drag will probably not represent as steep a cost as paying a stock picker, it's still a cost—and portfolio management alone can't help you completely mitigate this risk.

Finally, portfolio management risks goal misalignment. When your primary focus is portfolio management, you're more likely to focus on—and worry about—things like expected returns, standard deviation, and alpha than you are on your larger personal and financial goals.

A traditional financial manager isn't going to consider building out an income floor and may be more likely to take the wrong amount of investment risk because they're more focused on your portfolio's performance than your goals.

Portfolio management puts the portfolio at the center of your financial plan, when in reality, your portfolio should be an engine that funds your Wants and Wishes.

The Nature of the Portfolio Management Game

Portfolio management differs from stock picking in that it is a game of both luck and skill.

There is still an element of luck when it comes to Portfolio Management because the focus remains on investing to grow wealth. The market will always have its ups and downs, and portfolios will grow or shrink accordingly.

However, portfolio management does involve a level of true skill, rather than the greater levels of chance associated with stock picking. While it doesn't take a ton of skill to buy a bunch of ETFs in the right proportions, there is more legitimate skill in this game than in the game of stock picking. For example, you need to know how and when to rebalance your portfolio.

You need to be able to control you own behavior, as well. If the market corrects, it takes a certain level of skill to hold the course, rather than giving in to the panic and selling.

Game #3: Wealth Management

Several years ago in the fall, I attended a conference for fee-only financial advisors. While there is, admittedly, a lot of boring stuff that goes on at these events, you occasionally learn something that completely changes the way you think.

That was the case for me at that event. The speaker I saw showed us a simple equation, but it was one that shook my entire worldview:

WEALTH MANAGEMENT = INVESTMENT MANAGEMENT + FINANCIAL PLANNING

The term "wealth management" is thrown around quite a lot, but what is it, really? Too often, it's just another term for portfolio management for people with lots and lots of money. Investment and portfolio managers use the term to signal that they cater to the well-heeled.

That is decidedly *not* what the above equation signifies. True wealth management is an entirely different type of game—and it's a game of skill.

The Goal of Wealth Management

Wealth management refers to a process or solution that maximizes the chances of a person (or family) successfully achieving their life and financial goals. Wealth management emerges from a combination of investment management and habitual financial planning, which we'll talk about in more depth in Chapter Eleven.

How You Play the Wealth Management Game

Here's how you play the game of Wealth Management. You'll see as we walk through these steps that wealth management is far more all-encompassing than either stock picking or portfolio management. These steps are what make wealth management a game of skill, rather than a game of chance.

First, you must articulate your values and your life and financial goals. Refer to Chapter Four for an overview of how to identify your values and start setting life and financial goals that are in alignment with those values.

Second, you must dedicate some of your assets to creating an income floor that will meet your Needs for life. Chapter Six explains exactly how and why to create an income floor, as well as what the benefits are.

Next, you must determine your need, willingness, and ability to bear risk in the investment portfolio you design to support your

Wants and Wishes. Too many people—including most advisors—skip this step, but it is a critical one!

You've probably taken a "risk tolerance" questionnaire of some kind already. These questionnaires typically ask eight to 15 questions designed to help you understand what your emotional and psychological response would be if your portfolio's value dropped significantly.

While this is useful, there's also a "garbage in, garbage out" problem at work here. As it turns out, we have a hard time fully understanding the realities of our relationship with risk, meaning the questionnaire isn't likely to provide you with useful information. And yet the majority of financial advisors rely solely on a tool like this!

This issue nagged at me for years. Finally, I discovered a much more rigorous approach to understanding how much investment risk a person should bear. Rather than just focusing on your willingness, this approach considers your need, your ability, *and* your willingness to bear risk!

Before we dig into this topic further, keep this critical fact about your relationship with investment risk in mind: We have competing objectives for our assets.

When it comes to our non-discretionary spending (our Needs), we tend to be pretty risk-averse. However, when it comes to our Wants and Wishes, the reward tends to be worth a greater level of risk. So, we don't have one singular "willingness" to bear risk—we have two!

Here's a quick overview of what your need, willingness, and ability to bear risk might look like.

- Determine your need to bear investment risk. Your **need** to bear investment risk is the amount of risk you need to shoulder to reach your financial goals. The need acts as the "connective tissue" between your plan and your portfolio. The only way to make this determination accurately is to use financial planning software.

The only way we can quantify your need to bear risk is by building your financial plan and then finding the right portfolio. This is a powerful step!

I continue to be astonished that most people in my industry don't include this step in their process. It simply involves running a Monte Carlo analysis on multiple different portfolios, then selecting the plan that maximizes your probability of success.

Take Joe and Jack as examples. Joe is retiring with $2 million but wants to be able to spend $5 million over the rest of his life. That means Joe needs to bear significant equity risk.

Jack is also retiring with $2 million but only plans to spend $3 million over the rest of his life. Jack needs to bear significantly less equity risk than Joe.

A simulation for Joe, for example, might show that he needs a portfolio that is 90% stocks to maximize his chances of success, whereas Jack's portfolio only needs to be 40% stocks.

You can even run risk analyses yourself. All you must do is get your hands on some planning software, load in your goals and resources, and test out a few portfolios.

However, none of this information comes through in a risk tolerance questionnaire! Everyone's needs are so individualized that we can only derive real insight from financial planning software that runs a Monte Carlo analysis.

- Determine your willingness to bear investment risk. Your **willingness** to bear risk refers to your psychological and emotional response to gyrations in the value of your portfolio.

  How much of a dip can you tolerate before you start to panic and make poor decisions?

  You can get a better understanding of your

willingness to bear risk through discussion with a financial advisor or through examining maximum loss statistics. This is also the situation where the risk tolerance questionnaire is most useful—just remember that it's only one piece of the puzzle, rather than the whole picture!

- Your **ability** to bear risk includes your time horizon, flexibility in income and spending, the wealth effect, and the robustness of your income floor.

  Most retirees have a relatively low ability to bear investment risk, which is why conventional wisdom encourages you to be more conservative when you retire—but it isn't that simple.

  Take Suzy and Jane as examples here. Suzy is 40 and plans to retire in 20 years. Jane is 62 and retiring now. Both Suzy and Jane got the same score on their willingness to bear risk, but their situations are vastly different.

  Suzy plans to work for another 20 years, which means her ability to bear risk is much stronger than Jane's, whose plan needs to kick into action immediately. However, what if Jane is also willing to go back to work, or to cut her spending? Even though Jane plans to retire now, her willingness to make adjustments can change her ability to handle risk.

  Now take Peter. Peter is 70, and he's already retired. He has $10 million in his portfolio, but only spends $150,000 per year. Compared to his spending, his assets are so high that Peter has the ability to be 100% in stocks. However, if his spending increased to $350,000 per year his ability to bear risk would change and he might end up in a more traditional portfolio.

While some aspects of ability can be incorporated into a questionnaire, many cannot. This is why you need to use your best judgment and work with an advisor who understands that need, willingness, and ability should all be taken into consideration.

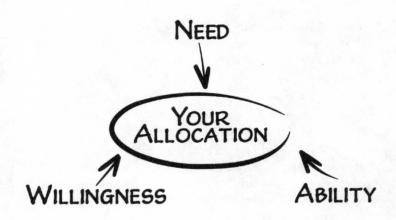

After you've assessed your need, willingness, and ability to bear risk, you can do what I call "setting your big slider" on your investment portfolio.

I'm sure by now you've seen all sorts of complicated charts showing the dozen or so asset classes and the various recommended percentages—those are not what I'm talking about here.

Those complex charts are popular in the marketing materials in the financial advice industry, in part because they make investing seem scientific. All those slices of pie and all those percentages give the illusion of serious thinking.

You don't need to get sucked into that. If you talk to 10 advisors, you'll get 10 different percentages for the various sub-asset classes—and there's no way to tell ahead of time who will be proven right and who will be proven wrong.

Your Big Slider

0% Stocks   60% Stocks   100% Stocks

Your big slider might look something like this. Put as simply as possible, your big slider refers to your chosen mix of stocks and bonds. In this example, it's the classic 60/40 split: 60% stocks and 40% bonds.

Your need, willingness, and ability to bear risk might move that slider towards one end or the other.

For example, if your need is for 50% stocks but your willingness to bear risk is a bit higher, I'd recommend setting the slider according to your need first. You might not have ever calculated your need to bear risk before—but it is where you should begin.

If your need is for 50% stocks but you *want* 70% stocks because you want the potential upside for yourself or your heirs, that's also a consideration. But you should still start with your need and err in favor of need over willingness.

NERDING OUT!

The important thing is to own all the stocks across all the asset classes, to assess your need, willingness, and ability to bear risk, and to set the slider accordingly.

Once you've set your big slider, you need to deploy your portfolio in a tax efficient fashion. We'll talk a lot more about taxes in Chapter Ten and focus on the difference between tax preparation and tax planning.

The final step of wealth management is aligning your portfolio with your estate plan. This involves getting all your beneficiary settings correct across all your accounts, as well as titling your accounts (or funding your trust) correctly. This is another step that lots of people skip, but it is another important one!

The Cost of Wealth Management

You can certainly play the Wealth Management game by yourself, but it takes time and study. I'll talk more about this in Chapter Thirteen.

You could ask a wealth manager to play this game for you. The cost of professional wealth management typically runs 1% of your total portfolio. It amazes me that the cost of stock picking is about the same as true wealth management, considering you are getting so much more with wealth management. What a bizarre industry!

With that said, 1% could still be a huge number depending on the size of your portfolio, and that 1% is connected to all sorts of conflicts of interest. Fortunately, there are also wealth management financial advisors who only charge a flat fee. I'll describe these issues and costs further in Chapter Thirteen.

Wealth management requires an investment on your part—but also provides significantly better returns than the previous two games.

The Risk of Wealth Management

All investing activities come with risks, but wealth management is the least risky of the three types of games discussed in this chapter and in Chapter Seven. In fact, the wealth management game mitigates several risks present in stock picking and portfolio management games. Wealth management:

1. Reduces the risks of counterproductive behavior

2. Explicitly aligns assets with your goals and preferences

3. Creates buffer assets

The two risks that you will still bear are stock market risk and the risk that your own behavior will sabotage your plan. We cannot control the outcomes of the stock market. Wealth management alleviates some of this risk by ensuring you have an income floor that will meet your Needs, and that your overall financial life is in good shape.

We can also learn to control our own behaviors to ensure that we don't sabotage our plans. One way to build buffers around our own behavior is by outsourcing wealth management to an advisor.

The Nature of the Wealth Management Game

Wealth management is largely a game of skill, and this is in part because wealth management is much more all-encompassing than the previous two games. There's a common saying: Personal finance is 80% personal. That truth shows up at its best in the wealth management game, which considers every aspect of your financial life and goals—not just your portfolio.

Playing the wealth management game also brings in tax planning (a topic we'll cover more in Chapter Ten), integrative thinking, and testing plan resilience.

Rather than focusing on which individual security you have a good gut feeling about, wealth management focuses on weaving your goals, tax planning, and income planning together into financial strategies that will help you retire with a feeling of relaxed confidence.

Wealth management enables you to test the resilience of your financial plan—a concept we talked about in Chapter Five—and address any weaknesses you find. This testing is based on a holistic understanding of your portfolio along with your goals, rather than focusing on portfolio performance alone.

The Game I Want You to Play

As I'm sure I've made clear in the preceding sections, I believe that the right game for all individual investors is the game of wealth management. This argument is based on logic, evidence, and my own professional experience.

Of the three games I've described, the game of wealth management is the one that takes the most skill. It's also the game that gives you the most control over the outcome, maximizing the chances that you will achieve your life and financial goals.

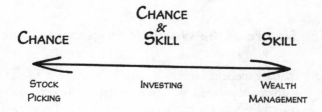

Wealth management is more complicated than the other games because you need to juggle more variables, but it is certainly worth it! We will talk more about how to get help with it (whether you decide to do it yourself or hire someone) in Chapter Thirteen.

Here's another way to think about these three games, which puts a slightly different spin on the relationships between them:

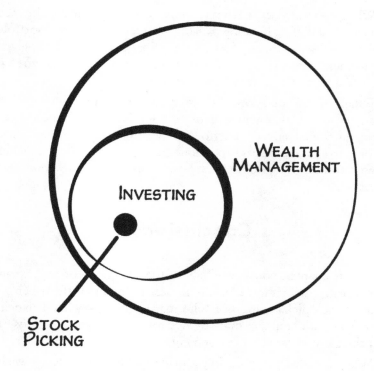

Stock picking is a small piece of the picture, within the broader picture of investing and portfolio management, which is itself only a portion of what wealth management truly means.

When you think about the three investing games this way, it becomes clearer that *you* get to decide where to place your attention, your focus, and your money.

You get to make the decision—not the media, not your friends, not your current advisor. You get to choose where to place your attention and decide which game you want to play.

Stock picking is the smallest portion in this model for good reason. Stock picking should play a small role in your financial life and be undertaken with the understanding that it (on average) cannot accomplish anything that your low-cost index fund or ETF portfolio can't.

When you move away from thinking of stock picking as the most important skill for building wealth, you can focus on portfolio management as a strategy for reducing financial risk without giving up expected returns. Portfolio management can become an important part of your overall financial strategy.

Finally, when you adopt a wealth management perspective, you'll begin to realize that you can drive your life and financial goals through your entire portfolio. Wealth management both encompasses and outclasses portfolio management *and* stock picking when it comes to providing the relaxed confidence you want in your retirement.

Conclusions

In this chapter, you learned about the true game of skill: wealth management, which includes all the best elements of the other two games (stock picking and portfolio management)—while balancing their risks with strategic thinking. I strongly urge you to choose to play the game of wealth management.

With that said, there is still a place within your overall wealth management game for stock picking! In the next chapter, we'll look at the idea of a Core and Explore portfolio, where most of your money is in boring ETFs and similar funds, but you dedicate a small percentage of your portfolio to stock picking and other goodies.

Key Takeaways

- **Wealth management:** A process or solution that maximizes the chances of successfully achieving life and financial goals. A combination of investment management and in-depth financial planning.

- Key steps for the game of wealth management:
  - Articulate your values and set life and financial goals
  - Dedicate some of your assets to creating an income floor
  - Determine your need, ability, and willingness to bear risk
  - Set your overall asset allocation
  - Deploy your portfolio in the most tax-efficient ways possible
  - Align your portfolio with a thorough estate plan

- The cost of wealth management can run about 1% of your total portfolio; you can also find flat fee financial advisors.

- Wealth management mitigates many of the risks of stock picking and portfolio management.

- The right game for individual investors is the game of wealth management. Wealth management gives you the most control over the outcome.

9. Going Exploring

Jack Bogle was a titan in the investment business.

Bogle founded the investment advising firm Vanguard and is credited with creating the index fund. Not only that, but Bogle also shone a big bright light on a lot of junk in the investment business. He fought for the little guy.

The passion and reverence shown by some of his disciples motivated them to create a community—even a movement—known as the Bogleheads. The Bogleheads emphasize living within your means, investing in low-cost index funds, and staying the course in your investment plan regardless of what the market is doing.

I'm proud to call myself a Boglehead and consider Jack Bogle one of my heroes.

So, you can imagine my dismay when I learned that Bogle had invested his own money with a stock picker! Not only that, but the stock picker was using an actively managed and expensive mutual fund with an expense ratio *30 times higher* than the typical Vanguard expense ratio.

How could the founder of Vanguard, the leader of low-cost investing, possibly betray his own principles like this? Was Bogle just another hypocrite in the filthy business of investing? I found myself wondering what the heck was going on.

Luckily, I managed to pass through the stages of grief pretty quickly. I was initially in denial that my hero would do such a thing—but the facts were the facts, and my denial couldn't last long. I moved through anger, bargaining, and depression, and landed on acceptance once I had all the facts about what was going on with Jack Bogle.

It turned out that Bogle was investing with his son. Jack Bogle, Jr. was running an actively managed small cap mutual fund, and his father wanted to support him.

Bogle, Sr. explained his reasoning clearly enough: "We do some things for family reasons. If it's not consistent, well, life isn't always consistent."[55]

That was enough for me! Learning the truth about Bogle's apparent inconsistency also shines a light on another truth about investing decisions: as Bogle said, life isn't always consistent!

We can know that the ideal portfolio is composed of low-cost index funds or ETFs—but the real world isn't ideal. Things can be a little more complicated than that. If Jack Bogle's finances shifted because of his family situation, anyone's can.

And that's not necessarily a bad thing. In this chapter, we'll talk about how you can have the perfect portfolio *and* leave room for life's complexities.

Lighten Up Already!

I learned about the perfect portfolio from Professor Bill Sharpe one beautiful spring day in Palo Alto, and that conversation changed the way I saw things forever. Sharpe left quite an impression on me!

The perfect portfolio is amazing in its simplicity, and it can be powered with nothing more than a set of ETFs. The perfect portfolio has a set of attributes that I call the Pillars of Portfolio Perfection.

In one streamlined, efficient package, you can achieve rock bottom expenses, supreme tax efficiency, massive amounts of diversification, and outstanding liquidity. For years and years, I simply could not wrap my head around the fact that anyone would want to deviate from this portfolio.

---

[55] Pleven, L. (2013).

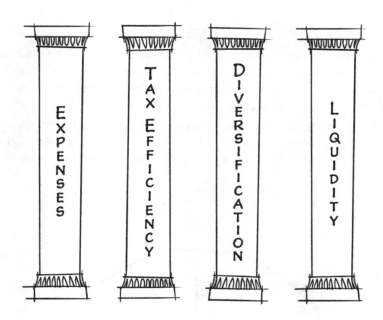

Thanks to the Pillars of Portfolio Perfection, I expect this type of portfolio to continue to outperform 80-85% of fund managers. Why would anyone use anything other than this portfolio when the chances of losing to it are five to six times greater than your chances of beating it?

Not only that, but *any* investment idea you can propose will compromise at least one of the Pillars of Portfolio Perfection. Anything else will cost more, have less diversification, be less tax efficient, and/or offer less liquidity. It's also going to be more complicated than anything that matches the Pillars. There's no way around it!

Early in my career, my colleagues used to tease me for being robotic. They often said I came across as coldly clinical, logical, and efficient. I thought it was funny at the time—but I look back on those comments now and realize that sometimes I was so focused on the logical answer that I truly couldn't understand the deviations. I couldn't understand the very human motivations that prompted them.

Then I learned about Jack Bogle and his son.

Bogle's inconsistency got me thinking more deeply about investment portfolios and why people make the choices they do. Over time, I realized that a Core and Explore approach could work well for some people—perhaps even most people!

Core and Explore refers to an investing approach where most of your investment portfolio, the Core, sits in low-cost ETFs. However, another section of your portfolio, your Explore portion, serves other purposes.

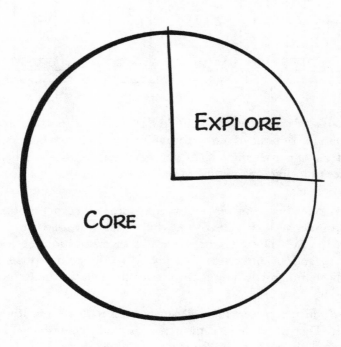

Don't get me wrong, I still think the "own all the stocks" portfolio is amazing for most people, and it should be the foundation of your overall investment strategy. But if you really want to Explore other types of investments with 10 to 20% of your portfolio, go for it!

Bogle inadvertently gave me (and all of us) an important gift by investing in his son's fund. He gave us permission to express ourselves in our portfolios—if we feel the need to. If Jack Bogle can do it, we can do it.

What started to really intrigue me is the *why*. What motivates some of us to Explore with our investments?

Why Do Explorers Explore?

I've traveled a fair amount, and I consider myself a true explorer. Here are some of the things that motivate true explorers:

- Looking for adventure

- Seeking wealth

- Discovering and learning

- Wanting to experience new things

- Testing their personal limits

I see all these motivations in Core and Explore approaches to investing, as well.

I've seen a lot of different reasons that actual portfolios deviate from the perfect Vanguard ETF portfolio, but I'd argue that there are nine central motivations. Review this list of motivations and see which ones, if any, might capture your motivations for wanting to slice off an Explore section of your portfolio.

Motivation #1: You Have No Choice

Lots of people have company stock these days, and some of that stock can't be sold. If you literally can't sell it because it hasn't vested yet (incentive stock options, non-qualified options, restricted stock units, and so on), then there is nothing you can do about it. You are being forced to Explore with part of your portfolio.

But if you own stock that has vested and you haven't sold it, that's an entirely different matter. As a rule, I like to see people diversify out of company stock as quickly as they can.

Your wages are already tied to this company; why should your assets be? The only potential exception here are incentive stock options (ISOs); if you have ISOs, you may want to exercise and then hold for one year before selling. This strategy allows you to enjoy lower long-term capital gains treatment.

There are several cognitive biases at play that explain why people unnecessarily hold stock in their employer:

- Some people are overly optimistic about their company's prospects; I find this is especially common among startup workers. The halo effect happens when positive feelings about a company affect your feelings or behavior in another area—enjoying where you work doesn't necessarily mean their stock is a good investment!

- Some people are over-confident about their ability to significantly influence the stock price. Your performance at work is unlikely to move the needle as much as you might assume.

- Some people demonstrate the endowment effect, a bias toward valuing things we own much more than other people do. If you already own company stock (or any stock!), it's likely you place more value on it than someone else would; that does not mean the stock is likely to perform better!

If you find that you might be falling prey to one of these cognitive biases, it's time to start thinking about diversification, even within the Explore portion of your portfolio!

If you have no choice but to hold company stock, then make the best of the situation and ensure it's only a small percentage of your overall portfolio.

Motivation #2: A Massive Potential Tax Bill

Maybe you own some securities in a taxable account that have appreciated significantly. Selling these assets is going to result in a fortune in taxes, simply because of that appreciation.

While the perfect portfolio approach would have you sell them off to put all your money with Vanguard or DFA, you don't need perfection—you just need a strategy that is good enough, and that is responsive to the actual circumstances of your individual portfolio.

If you have highly appreciated assets, you can continue to hold them to avoid the capital gains taxes. You can consider selling the assets slowly, so that the tax burden is distributed across time. As these assets are sold, the money you collect can be added into the Core portfolio, moving you closer to the north star of the perfect portfolio.

Motivation #3: Expressing Your Values

Responsible investing has become increasingly popular in recent years, often in the form of Environmental, Social, and Governance (ESG) investing. It's sometimes also referred to as socially responsible investing (SRI).

ESG scores are primarily focused on sustainability,[56] including assessments of how environmentally friendly and socially conscious an organization is.[57] Some scores include internal and external measurements, as well as assessments of leadership diversity and executive pay.

ESG investing is taking "vote with your dollars" to a whole new level, allowing investors to look for returns from organizations that have the kind of social impact they prefer.

The US SIF Foundation reports that $17.1 trillion had been invested using sustainable strategies at the start of 2020—that is a full third of the $54.1 trillion of assets under management in the U.S.

Another option, especially if significant charitable giving is one of your Wishes, is to use highly appreciated assets as the basis of a donor-advised fund. If you give appreciated stock to such a fund, you don't have to pay capital gains taxes.

From there, you can direct that money to be distributed from the fund to eligible 501(c)(3) charities of your choice over a lengthy period.

NERDING OUT!

---

[56] Clark, G. L., Feiner, A., & Viehs, M. (2015).
[57] Lomax, A. and Rotonti, J. (2021).

alone![58] ESG investing is far from a fringe approach.

ESG ETFs are available across a range of platforms. While investing in the total stock market still provides the most beneficial and diversified portfolio, ESG funds provide opportunities for investors to support companies and causes they feel aligned with.

Motivation #4: Vegas, Baby!

Tens of millions of people flock to Las Vegas every year for one reason: to be entertained. Fortunately, most visitors to Vegas are only looking for entertainment and know the game is rigged. They decide how much money they can afford to lose for the weekend, and they stick to it.

I recommend opening what I like to call the "Vegas Account" if you're interested in playing the stock picking game and taking a gamble with a small slice of your money. The Vegas Account is typically a dedicated IRA where you buy and sell individual stocks. I strongly recommend using an IRA for this type of account, since there are no tax consequences if you sell a position with a gain.

If you want to trade stocks and are willing to admit that you have no idea how your picks will perform, I encourage you to slice off 5 to 10% of your portfolio into your Vegas Account and go for it, as long as you set clear parameters around it.

One of my clients, for example, decided to invest $150,000 of his portfolio into cryptocurrency. A new retiree, Gary simply enjoyed feeling like he still had some skin in the game. While 85% of his portfolio stayed in safe, boring investments, he sectioned off 15% for what we came to call his Vegas Account.

Acknowledging the money as the Vegas Account helped Gary set reasonable parameters for how much risk he was willing to take, how diversified he wanted to be within the Vegas Account, and whether he would use an IRA or a taxable account (depending on whether he wanted to actively trade or buy and hold).

---

[58] US SIF (2020).

Building a Vegas Account like this is helpful because it keeps you humble, helps you set and stick to your limits, and ensures that you're still able to have fun!

Motivation #5: Friends and Family

I see lots of ETF investors who will nevertheless throw $25,000 to $50,000 at a restaurant a buddy is opening. Other investors will go in on a college roommate's hedge fund, or angel invest in their own kid's fledgling company.

I work with many, many investors who won't sell stock they've inherited from their parents out of loyalty and sentimentality.

Patrick, a client of mine, received a $300,000 payout from a deferred compensation plan. After paying taxes, he decided to invest all of it in a tech startup run by someone he knew. Risking close to $300,000 on a single startup might sound like an unconscionable risk—but for Patrick, it represented only a small portion of his $5 million portfolio, the rest of which was in a diversified fund that met his Needs and was well positioned to fund his Wants and Wishes.

When Patrick presented the idea to me, I said, "Sure," and that was the end of the conversation. I didn't push back. I didn't do any research evaluating the startup. Here's why: There's no way to predict whether any one startup will succeed or fail.

Additionally, swinging for the fences and risking striking out also wouldn't impact the stability of Patrick's overall financial plan—the risk was immaterial. But making that investment allowed him to explore by supporting his friend's company.

This friends and family motivation is exactly what Jack Bogle was talking about when he explained why his funds were being actively managed. He had no problem joining the other team because the other team was his son.

Setting aside a small portion of your portfolio to support friends and family allows you to be generous without disrupting your Core portfolio.

Motivation #6: Addressing Specific Risks

Let's say you have an ETF portfolio that's 70% Stocks and 30% Bonds, and let's further assume that the 70/30 split was based a rigorous process that analyzed your need, willingness, and ability to bear risk.

This portfolio is well protected against inflation because it's composed of 70% stocks. It is incredibly well diversified because it has all the asset classes and all the stocks. The portfolio also has an overall level of risk that is appropriate to your financial plan.

But imagine that you are concerned about *one specific risk*. You might be concerned about...

- Inflation. If inflation is a worry, you might insist that your bonds offer explicit inflation protection as well.

  In that case, you could own a bunch of Treasury Inflation Protected Securities (TIPS). Or maybe you want to disproportionately own the types of stocks that offer the best inflation protection, or commodities.

- The total value of your portfolio falling. If you're worried about the overall value of your portfolio, you might buy options on the stock market to protect your downside. This is very expensive, but some people do it.

- Diversification. You might worry about diversification so much that owning all the stocks isn't enough.

  Maybe you want to try to squeeze a little more blood from the diversification stone by owning more real estate investment trusts (REITs). You might also want to add diversity in the form of commodities.

Motivation #7: Getting Real

Some people are motivated to explore by investing in real estate, which I can understand. Real estate has produced great wealth in this country, and it certainly feels safer than stocks (although whether that's true or not is open to debate[59]) because it is tangible and because you don't see the value gyrating wildly every day.

Many real estate investors do well in this arena because they choose to purchase good property in growing areas, and they focus on long-term rental or vacation rental activities.

An investment property is not the same as an investment portfolio in the same way that an index fund would be, however.

Real estate requires much more active management—sometimes literally, if you decide to forgo the cost of a property management company and get involved in repairs and upkeep yourself.

The key benefit of investment properties is that they can serve as a kind of cash reserve. Renting the property out adds to your regular monthly cash flow, sometimes significantly, especially if the mortgage is fully paid off.

Additionally, an investment property can be an emergency cash fund: should the market really take a tumble, and you find yourself in need of additional financial support, you can always sell the property.

If you are going to buy and own investment real estate, be sure to research relevant laws and tax implications in your state, explore the costs and benefits of hiring a property management company, and take your time choosing the right property to buy. A good real estate agent should be able to guide you on finding investment property.

---

[59] Voigt, K. (2021).

Motivation #8: Affinity and Loyalty

Brands can hold incredible sway over us. Many brands happily extract a brand premium from us, and we are happy to pay it! There are countless examples of the brand premium from all walks of our lives. Here are a couple of examples I've seen in my own work.

I offered to analyze the portfolio of a recent prospective client. He owned 12 Fidelity mutual funds—held, of course, at Fidelity. Our software showed that what he owned was the functional equivalent of a Vanguard ETF portfolio: all the same asset classes in all the same percentages.

But his Fidelity portfolio was *10 times* as expensive as the Vanguard equivalent. If you walked into a supermarket and saw a $35 gallon of milk next to a gallon of identical quality that cost $3.50, which are you more likely to choose?

Another client, who'd left her job at McKinsey two decades before we spoke, refused to roll over her 401(k) because it was offered through McKinsey. She saw the 401(k) as her remaining link to the company, even though it would have been more advantageous to move it.

Some affluent investors invest in hedge funds. Is this because they offer returns greater than their risks…or because these investors get to travel in the rarefied air of the well-branded hedge fund manager and the rest of their well-heeled clientele?

The traditional hedge fund wants 2% of your investment every year, plus 20% of the upside! Warren Buffet was so appalled by this that he bet a hedge fund manager that hedge funds as a category would lose to the S&P 500. Buffet won the bet. Yet many people continue to invest in hedge funds.

Brand loyalty can encourage us to make illogical decisions, and that loyalty is often personal and deeply felt.

If there's a brand, company, or approach you feel strongly about, you can pursue it—just make sure it's not to the detriment of your overall portfolio.

Motivation #9: A Strong Conviction

Strong conviction is the most dangerous motivation for Exploring.

A strong conviction can persuade you to believe that you have an insight that other investors don't.

You believe your prediction is likely to be accurate. You believe you can identify investments with returns greater than their risks. You believe that your analysis or research or instincts or observations—or those of your friend, or those of a professional investor you follow—will lead you to beat the stock market.

Or maybe you believe you can time the market. That one's tough because you need to be right twice, knowing when to get out and when to get back in. Being right once is hard enough!

If you hold a strong conviction that a certain investment (or investment guru) offers returns greater than its risks, feel free to explore, but put some parameters around your exploration!

Being a Good Explorer

If you decide to pursue a Core and Explore approach, please practice the following habits for keeping yourself—and your retirement financial plan—safe:

- Create separation. Decide up front what percentage of your portfolio will be Core (the boring, low-cost diversified investments like Vanguard ETFs), and what percentage will be focused on exploration. Separate your Explore money into a different account (or accounts) from your Core money.

- Understand your why. Try to figure out your motivations. There are a lot of reasons we might be tempted to Explore. What's driving you? How should that motivation shape what you do with that Explore fund?

- Keep expenses and taxes in mind. If you find yourself tempted by any investment opportunity that comes with high expenses, you had better have a *lot* of conviction! A sexy-sounding private equity investment that wants 2% every year plus 20% of the upside isn't a good deal.

  The investment might outperform your Core portfolio, but those fees are going to eat up a lot of your potential gains. And if an investment manager churns your account, you could pay all sorts of taxes at terribly unpleasant rates!

- Eat your free lunch. The only free lunch in investing is diversification, so it's much better to be a diversified explorer—someone who visits all sorts of places—than to home in on a single destination.

  That is, don't go all in on a single stock, but find a way to introduce diversification even into your Explore investment portfolio.

Conclusions

I believe the perfect portfolio exists—but that doesn't mean that's the only portfolio you're allowed to have. Life is complicated and perfection, frankly, can become a little boring after a while. It's possible to develop a Core and Explore portfolio that will provide for your Wants and Wishes while also allowing you to stay actively engaged with your money, take some risks, and maybe hit it big.

At this point, we've discussed the importance of resilience and understanding risk, how to create an income floor, the differences between stock picking, portfolio management, and wealth management, and Core and Explore portfolios. Now, it's time to talk about everyone's favorite subject: taxes.

Key Takeaways

- Jack Bogle's investment philosophy shapes mine, so I was dismayed to learn that Bogle's own money was invested with a stock picker—until I learned the stock picker was his son. Life is complex; sometimes our investment choices are too.

- **Core and Explore:** Most of your investment portfolio (the Core) sits in low-cost ETFs. A smaller percentage (the Explore) is dedicated to deviations and calculated risk-taking.

- Keep yourself safe when Exploring by:
  - Creating clear separation between your Core and Explore portfolios.
  - Understanding your motivations for Exploring and making choices in alignment with those driving forces.
  - Keeping taxes and expenses in mind.
  - Eating your free lunch and ensuring you have diversification across the board.

- The perfect portfolio does exist—but that doesn't mean it's the only portfolio you're allowed to have!

10. Taxes & Retirement

When my wife told me she was pregnant with our first child, I was thrilled. I felt both excited and nervous, like any new father-to-be. I did all the usual things: hugged my wife and expressed my joy.

Then I did something that might seem a little unusual to most people: I wrote the state of Utah a check for $140,000. We lived in Virginia at the time—I'd never set foot in Utah, nor did I owe the state of Utah any money. So, you might be asking, what gives?

What would prompt me to hand over $140,000 to another state before we'd even told anyone we were going to have a baby?

Well, here's the thing. Utah has an amazing 529 plan, and I am always on the lookout for tax planning activities that will pay off in the long run. Super-funding my unborn child's 529 plan was just such an activity.

This chapter is all about thinking a little differently about taxes, as I did with the 529 plan and as many of my clients do. We'll talk later in the chapter about how to turn a 529 plan into a multi-generational wealth transfer machine.

In this chapter, we're going to start thinking broadly about how taxes relate to your ability to feel a sense of relaxed confidence in retirement. We'll look at the difference between tax preparation and tax planning and cover my favorite tax planning strategies.

A 529 plan is a tax-advantaged investment account for education-related funds—and can be used for K-12 educational expenses, college, skilled trades training, and student loan repayment.* Making a large one-time contribution to a 529 plan means that money will continue to grow, tax-free, until it's used.

*US Securities and Exchange Commission

NERDING OUT!

Thinking Big About Taxes

Most of us are passive when it comes to our taxes, even though we might not realize it. Sure, we file our taxes year in and year out. We're participating in our company's 401(k) plan and setting money aside for retirement. We get a tax break by doing so, and that's nice too. Maybe we're even planning a backdoor Roth strategy.

Big deal!

That's standard tax preparation behavior, and it's entirely too passive to get the results you will need and want for relaxed confidence in retirement. Before we look at specific tax planning strategies, we need to start thinking a little differently about taxes themselves.

A Big Number

In working with clients on wealth management, I've observed that most of my clients will wind up paying somewhere between $2 million and $5 million in taxes across their lifetime. That is not chump change, my friend!

It's time to take more ownership of your tax planning activities.

Thinking Differently About the Goal

If you're like most people, you probably think the goal is to avoid, minimize, or defer your tax burden. Sometimes this is the right approach—but limiting our thinking about taxes in this way too often puts us in a passive or even reactive stance.

The correct goal for your taxes is much more nuanced. The goal is not simply to avoid, minimize, or defer taxes.

The goal of tax planning is to maximize your after-tax wealth.

The absolute best book I read during my time in business school was called *The Goal*, and it was written by business management guru Eliyahu Goldratt.[60] One of Goldratt's key points in *The Goal* is that it's essential to set one single well-understood goal, and then to make all your decisions accordingly.

---

[60] Goldratt, E. (2012).

If you earn $200,000 a year, you'll pay $2 million in taxes over 50 years, assuming a 20% tax rate. If you earn $300,000 a year, across 60 years and assuming a 25% tax rate, you'll pay $4.5 million in taxes. I recommend you look at your own income, tax rate, and career trajectory, and think hard about how much you've already paid—and how much you might have left to pay.

Handing over $2 million to $5 million in nothing but taxes represents an immense drain on your retirement planning capabilities. Yet most of us continue to approach taxes in the most passive ways imaginable.

NERDING OUT!

That is, every single subsequent decision you make should be weighed in terms of whether that decision moves you closer to your goal or not.

If you must pick a single goal for dealing with your taxes, I propose that the goal should be shifting your focus from the "avoid, minimize, defer" approach to an approach dedicated to maximizing your after-tax wealth.

Let me help you understand why.

Once you've decided to focus on maximizing your after-tax future wealth, you can start making all your tax-related decisions with that goal in mind.

Your goal, to get a bit more detailed, should be maximizing your after-tax wealth, given your chosen level of investment risk, while also diversifying your tax risk.

This goal requires undertaking a fuller analysis of all available options when it comes to taxation. Rather than solely focusing on avoiding, minimizing, or deferring taxes, you might find that in some cases paying slightly more in taxes, or paying taxes sooner rather than later, results in that maximization.

Focusing on maximizing your after-tax wealth can require a challenging shift in mindset, but it is critical!

From the perspective of wealth management, reframing the tax conversation to focus on maximization is the only approach that makes sense. If you want to succeed at the wealth management game and retire with a sense of relaxed confidence, your job must become increasing your spending capabilities—not just passively reducing your tax bill.

Wealth management requires a more complex and nuanced approach than avoiding, minimizing, or deferring taxes.

Let's look at an example to see why this is so important. While this example is admittedly over-simplified, it gets to the heart of the issue.

Imagine you are presented with two investment opportunities: the Maximization option, which you'll pay some taxes on, and the Minimization option, which you won't. The Minimization approach would encourage you to select that option immediately, simply because it's tax-free.

Those of us who want to maximize our after-tax wealth will want to look more closely at each investment's rate of return, the tax rate, and the after-tax outcome.

	MAXIMIZE	MINIMIZE
RETURN	7%	3%
TAXES	2%	0%
NET RETURN	5%	3%

In this scenario, the Maximization option has a 7% gross return and requires paying 2% taxes, while the Minimization option has a 3% return with no taxes.

The after-tax net return is what's essential here. Yes, you'll pay 2% taxes on the Maximization option—but you are still left with a 5% after-tax return, which beats the Minimization's 3%. While these percentages seem small, those differences add up over time!

While this example is simplified to illustrate the concept, you'd be surprised at how many people make the mistake of choosing a minimization option even when the maximization option would leave them with greater returns in the long run!

Here's another example to help you think through the problem of minimization. Some life insurance agents are out there offering Life Insurance Retirement Plans (LIRPs). My take is that this is just a marketing gimmick designed to sell permanent life insurance (whole life and universal life).

The basic strategy looks something like this. The agent will tell you to:

1. Overfund the policy with significant premiums over time

2. Take loans against your policy to drive **tax-free** income

3. Leave any remaining death benefit to your heir(s), **tax free**

"Free" is one of the most powerful words in the English language—and I'm willing to bet that "tax" is one of the most hated.

Now, admittedly, a "tax-free retirement" sounds awesome. There are just a couple of problems.

First, the commission you'll wind up paying on these products can be so staggeringly high that you have to commit to the strategy for 15+ years just to have any hope at a decent return! You may think you're happy to do that if it means avoiding taxes—but the reality is that the insurance companies profit handsomely from people who believe they'll stick with a policy and then end up dropping it.

Second, the annual expenses on many of these contracts are upwards of 3%. Compare that to the annual expenses on index ETFs, which are often 0.1%, as mentioned in previous chapters. That means the expenses on these insurance contracts can be *30 times* the alternative. This massive difference in expenses wipes out the tax advantage and then some!

People who buy these policies are made to feel like they're doing the smart thing by "avoiding taxes." They are avoiding taxes—but they're also undermining the more important goal of maximizing after-tax wealth.

Another nuance to keep in mind is that LIRPs are often positioned as Roth alternatives. This is a massive sub-optimization of the principles of asset location, which we'll talk about later in this chapter. The best type of investment to put in a Roth is U.S. equities—*not* a conservative "investment" like a whole life insurance policy.

A good wealth manager can help you assess your options and make choices that maximize your after-tax returns.

The Life Insurance Pitch for Retirement

Focusing on maximizing after-tax returns should become a core part of your approach to taxes as you plan for a retirement characterized by a sense of relaxed confidence.

Unfortunately, many people who take the avoid, minimize, or defer approach fall for permanent life insurance pitches. Life insurance salespeople present permanent life insurance as a great option: after all, it's tax-free!

The problem is that permanent life insurance is generally a distraction from the true goal of maximizing your usable wealth. The extra costs often overwhelm the tax advantage.

The pitch you'll hear from such salespeople is that the growth on permanent life insurance is tax-free, which sounds alluring. However, if you look at the performance between permanent life insurance and term life insurance, the numbers tell a different story.

The truth is that you're almost always going to be better off buying term life insurance and investing the difference. Yes, you'll wind up paying a bit in taxes with this approach—but you'll accumulate a greater amount of after-tax wealth.

This is exactly why focusing on maximizing your after-tax returns needs to be at the core of all your tax-related activities, rather than working to avoid, minimize, or defer what you pay. Unfortunately, people fall for the minimizing approach all the time because it sounds attractive to pay no taxes. Such people wind up with smaller portfolios and a decreased ability to fund their Wants and Wishes in retirement.

Whether you complain about taxes or regard paying taxes as part of your civic duty, keep in mind that your chief goal must be maximizing your own portfolio!

With that out of the way, let's turn our attention to the difference between tax preparation and tax planning, and why that difference matters. After that, we'll look at a few powerful tax planning ideas that will set you up to both reduce your tax liability *and* maximize your after-tax returns.

Tax Preparation vs. Tax Planning

In addition to shifting your mindset to one of maximizing after-tax returns, it's also important to recognize the difference between tax preparation and tax planning.

Tax preparation is what most of us think about when we think about taxes: the boring slog of gathering and filling out all the forms, preparing your income return, filing everything, and waiting for a refund or writing a check to the IRS.

There's typically quite a bit of grumbling associated with tax preparation. It's a process we all go through, whether we do it ourselves or pay someone to take it off our plates. When we focus on tax preparation, we're often thinking about how we can reduce what we'll hand over to Uncle Sam or making plans for the money we'll get in our refund.

Tax preparation is required. It's a tactical, backward-looking activity that is focused on the reality of the past year's influence on your financial situation.

Tax planning, on the other hand, is a strategic analysis of your financial situation and the creation of a plan that ensures all elements work together to both reduce your tax liability *and* maximize your ability to make contributions to retirement plans and increase your after-tax returns.

Tax planning is optional. Because it's strategic, not everyone does it. Tax planning is a forward-looking activity that allows you to ask "what if?" questions that can dramatically increase your after-tax wealth.

Too many of us get stuck on thinking about ways to reduce what we owe and forget that maximizing returns can have a much more significant long-term impact on retirement accounts and finances in retirement.

Tax Prep	Tax Planning
Required	Optional
Tactical	Strategic
Looking Back	Looking Forward
Reality	What If?

With that in mind, here are seven of my favorite tax planning ideas for people approaching retirement or who are already retired. Depending on the specifics of your situation, these strategies can create more than $1 million in after-tax wealth!

Think of it this way: you can continue to engage in passive tax preparation activities and pay $2 million to $5 million in taxes—or you can start to get strategic with tax planning and generate $1 million or more in wealth.

Strategy 1: Lock It in Now

You've probably built up a significant balance in your pretax accounts like your IRAs and 401(k)s. Once you reach retirement, the next step should be to launch an aggressive multi-year Roth Conversion campaign.

The Roth Conversion works like this: Take money out of your IRA and put it into your Roth IRA. As a reminder, the key difference between a traditional and a Roth IRA all comes down to taxation. When using a traditional IRA, you deduct contributions immediately and pay taxes later; a Roth IRA requires tax payments immediately, but you get tax-free withdrawals later.

This arrangement is what makes the Roth Conversion strategy such an essential one for maximizing your after-tax returns.

Take John and Cynthia. When they came to my office, they were 56 years old, planning to retire, and had $5 million in pre-tax IRAs alone. They wouldn't need to touch that $5 million for several years, which meant it was going to continue to grow.

Here's what will happen when John and Cynthia turn 72, though: if they leave all that money in the IRAs, the IRS is going to force them to start taking required minimum distributions (RMD). The size of the RMD is based on a percentage, based on IRS actuarial tables related to life expectancy, and the percentage grows every year after age 72.

That means John and Cynthia could wind up having to take

hundreds of thousands of dollars out of their IRAs every year—whether or not they need to—and pay income taxes on it. Due to our progressive income tax regime, they would be forced into higher and higher tax brackets.

Additionally, whichever spouse outlives the other will be forced into an even higher tax bracket because filing as a single person is much more expensive than if you're married and filing jointly. If you look at the reality of our current demographics, recent history, and put tax rates in historical context, you'll see that taxes in the present moment are extremely low. It's much more likely that taxes will go up than down.

While IRAs are useful tools, they can also become a ticking time bomb. The good news is that a Roth Conversion allows you to start to defuse that bomb. John and Cynthia had a 16-year window to do their Roth Conversion, which had them move about $300,000 each year from a pre-tax IRA to a Roth IRA. They paid taxes on the money they moved, but at a much lower and more manageable rate than if they'd waited for RMDs to kick in.

For the majority of my clients, there are several key reasons for embarking on a multi-year Roth Conversion campaign, and for choosing to fill up the 22% tax bracket for each year of that campaign. Many go into 24% or even fill up 24%.

First, like John and Cynthia, you'll have to pay taxes on any withdrawals from your traditional IRA, as well as on any contributions you originally deducted from your taxes. While triggering a taxable event like this might sound like a bad idea, the benefits far outweigh the taxes you'll pay.

This is because once that money gets converted into your Roth IRA, all your subsequent growth and withdrawals are tax-free! This strategy helps you lock in a low rate of taxation on your traditional IRA money now, as opposed to exposing your portfolio to a much higher rate of taxation later.

Bracketology

Let's say that a long-range analysis clearly shows that Lisa and Tom should fill-up the 22% bracket with Roth Conversion dollars. Just look up the top of the 22% bracket ($185,000 as of 2022) and calculate how many Roth dollars it will take to bring you to the top of the bracket. When you execute the Roth Conversion, you should move the securities that have the most growth potential into your Roth.

NERDING OUT!

The next reason to embark on an aggressive Roth Conversion strategy is that Roth IRAs have no RMDs. Your money can simply continue to grow and grow, and you can leave it there for as long as you want. Starting the Roth Conversion process means that you are reducing your tax liability for the future!

Third, having a Roth Conversion strategy increases your tax diversification. Although we most often think of diversification in terms of our investment portfolios, it's equally important when it comes to our tax strategy.

Tax diversification involves spreading your money across a variety of different accounts with different tax characteristics. As it's impossible to predict how tax rates will change, tax diversification allows you to account for multiple possibilities.

The final reason for a strong Roth Conversion plan is that, as mentioned above, in the event of an early death, the surviving spouse will face significantly higher tax rates. Filing taxes as a single person rather than married filing jointly will increase the tax burden on a surviving spouse. Taking aggressive action on your Roth Conversion will reduce that tax burden should one of you die sooner than the other.

Most of the Roth Conversion decision comes down to your perspective on tax rates. If you believe your current tax rate is lower than your future tax rate is likely to be, then convert.

There are a couple of "hidden taxes" that sometimes pop up for people executing a Roth Conversion, and it is worth factoring them into your decision.

Take Mary. Mary is 65 and contemplating another Roth Conversion. She can convert at 22% and it seems like a bargain. However, now that Mary is 65, she's on Medicare. When you're on Medicare and your taxable income crosses a certain threshold, your premiums also jump up!

If Mary added $100,000 to her tax return, she would pay $22,000 in Federal taxes at the 22% tax rate. However, her Medicare costs would also increase by $3,000 as a direct result of that addition—meaning she's effectively paying $25,000 for the Roth Conversion.

Many people simply choose to do a smaller conversion in these situations. There are several thresholds like this, and you can size your Roth Conversion to convert just enough to avoid triggering the next Medicare premium increase.

Another hidden tax can show up for people who aren't yet on Medicare, but who have their own insurance through the Affordable Care Act (ACA). Bob retired early, at 55, and purchased ACA insurance coverage for $15,000 per year.

If Bob shows no income on his tax return, he will either be covered by Medicaid or will receive a Premium Tax Credit (PTC) for most of that $15,000. Bob is in a low tax bracket, which makes him a great candidate for a Roth Conversion. However, if he adds $100,000 to his tax return because of that conversion, his PTC falls significantly—meaning he's paying taxes on the conversion plus losing some of that PTC.

As you plan for retirement, mindful Roth Conversions mean you can take steps that will reduce your tax liability now and into the future while positioning your money to continue growing. The Roth Conversion process is a great plan for meeting those objectives!

Strategy 2: The Triple Play

The next tax planning strategy you should focus on is my favorite type of retirement account. While it's commonly referred to as a Health Savings Account (HSA), I'd argue this type of account is mislabeled. You should start to think of your HSA as an IRA—only better.

If you can get an HSA, do so immediately. If you're using your current HSA to pay medical expenses, stop that right now!

An HSA is the only account on the planet with a triple tax advantage: your money goes in pre-tax, grows in a tax-deferred account, and can be withdrawn tax-free for qualified medical expenses. After you turn 65, the money can be withdrawn tax-free for *any* purpose.

However, just contributing the maximum amount to your HSA each year isn't enough. You also have to move your contribution into an investment account within the HSA and then invest the funds.

Then continue funding that account and investing the money each year, and watching it grow—and grow!

Plan to leave these funds untouched until you turn 65. Funds in your HSA can then be ideal for creating your income floor or supporting your Wants and Wishes.

Strategy 3: What's Your Order?

A major part of tax planning is knowing that which account you pull from, and when, makes a big difference when it comes to your tax liability and after-tax returns.

For example, you might have tax-exempt accounts like a Roth IRA, taxable accounts like a brokerage account that you fund with after-tax money, and tax-deferred accounts like a 401(k), 403(b), or traditional IRA.

So how do you know what to pull from and when?

All these account types have different tax implications and will result in different taxes owed when you start drawing from them in retirement.

Fortunately, there's a relatively straightforward process you can follow to set up a withdrawal sequence that both reduces your overall tax liability and maximizes your after-tax returns. You'll want to develop a plan that first acknowledges the specific composition of your own income floor and investment portfolio.

The general withdrawal sequence to focus on is as follows:

- Taxable accounts first,
- Tax-deferred accounts second,
- Tax-exempt accounts last.

Drawing from your taxable accounts first means that tax-deferred and tax-exempt accounts have more time to continue growing, thus maximizing the amount of tax-free money in your overall portfolio.

Further, you'll pay capital gains and income taxes on taxable accounts, such as brokerage accounts, so it's wise to withdraw money from those accounts first. Remember that it's much more likely that taxes will increase than that they will decrease, so reducing your taxable burden in this way also maximizes your after-tax wealth.

Next, you'll want to begin focusing on tax-deferred accounts like your 401(k) or 403(b). You can blend this strategy with the Roth Conversion process discussed previously.

You will pay taxes when you withdraw money from your tax-deferred accounts, so it helps to take that money out early and reduce your overall tax burden. As with taxable accounts, focusing on tax-deferred accounts second also allows your tax-exempt accounts to continue growing and benefiting from compound interest.

Finally, you'll begin withdrawing from tax-exempt accounts like your Roth IRA or HSA. These accounts should be left for last precisely because they best achieve the dual goals of minimizing tax liability and—most important—maximizing growth.

Since tax-exempt accounts are typically funded with after-tax money (with the notable exception of the HSA's triple play), you've already paid the taxes. This means withdrawals are also tax-free.

Letting these accounts grow for as long as possible maximizes your returns in the most efficient way.

Strategy 4: Location, Location, Asset Location

Asset location is an important element of diversifying your portfolio across multiple asset classes and maximizing your after-tax wealth. Asset location differs from asset allocation.

Asset allocation refers to the percentage breakdown of your portfolio across stocks and bonds—picture the big slider discussed in Chapter Eight.

Asset *location* refers to the strategic placement of your assets across taxable and tax-sheltered accounts with the goal of increasing your returns.

Locating assets simply means owning each security in the correct account type—taxable, pre-tax, and Roth. REITs belong in a pre-tax category because they are tax inefficient and have higher expected returns. It's often beneficial to hold international stocks in taxable accounts to avail yourself of the Foreign Tax Credit. Bonds are tricky. When yields are high, bonds should be in pre-tax. When they are low, it doesn't matter where you place them. U.S. stocks can go anywhere, but try to place the securities with the highest growth potential (e.g., small caps or technology) in your Roth accounts.

Sometimes your hands are a bit tied. If you own highly appreciated positions in taxable accounts, but you "should" own them elsewhere, it is generally not worth realizing gains just to perfect your location. However, the results are worth the effort. According to Bob French at Retirement Researcher, good asset location can increase your returns by up to half a percentage point every year.[61]

Although half a percentage point might not sound like a significant amount of money, it works out to $500 for every $100,000 you have invested. The larger your overall portfolio, the more of a difference this strategy can make. If you have a $2 million portfolio, that works out to an additional $10,000 of growth every year!

Strategy 5: One and Done?

If you're anything like most of my clients, you are somewhat charitably inclined—and you want to make sure your donations are handled in the most efficient way possible. Should you plan to donate to charity, you might as well pair that with a tax planning strategy and

---

[61] French, B. (n. d.)

use a donor-advised fund.

The strategy here is to establish a donor-advised fund and then make a large, one-time contribution to the fund—typically, you'll want to use your most highly appreciated securities.

The result is that you get to write off the entire contribution at tax time, *and* you can then give money from the fund to designated charities in small amounts, for the rest of your life!

Let's use my clients Bruce and Lisa as an example. Lisa is a senior executive at a major tech company and wound up with a 50% concentrated position—half of the couple's $3 million portfolio was in her employer's stock. Lisa also happened to be quite charitably inclined, which meant that a donor-advised fund would help kill a few birds with one stone.

I helped Bruce and Lisa decide how much money they wanted to give to charities each year for the rest of their lives. They were in their 50s, and we assumed they had 40 more years of giving to do. Lisa wanted to give away $15,000 a year. Most people would just peel $15,000 out of their portfolio each year and give it away, getting a small tax write-off every time.

Instead, Lisa put $300,000 of her highly appreciated employer stock into a donor-advised fund. Doing this allowed her to simultaneously write that $300,000 off from her income taxes, avoid paying $60,000 in capital gains taxes, and reduce the concentrated position of her portfolio. Now, she can still give $15,000 a year while the donor-advised fund apparatus handles all the back-office administration.

Using a donor-advised fund provides wealth-maximizing benefits by allowing you to avoid capital gains taxes on the securities you contribute to the fund. It also provides you with a lifetime's worth of tax deductions all at once.

The best time to establish a donor-advised fund is before you retire, when you're likely to be in a higher tax bracket. This will further reduce your tax liability and allow all your other assets to continue growing.

However, setting up a donor-advised fund is a good strategy even if you've already retired. You can even accelerate your Roth Conversion strategy to take advantage of the large donor-advised fund deduction!

This path offers dual benefits: you reduce your tax liability and you increase the amount of money in your Roth IRA, which will then keep on growing tax-free.

Strategy 6: Let It Ride

As I mentioned at the beginning of this chapter, a 529 plan is a tax-advantaged investment account that allows a designated individual to use the funds to pay for educational expenses like college, K-12 tuition, apprenticeships, and student loans.

There are tax benefits for contributing to a 529 plan in many states, including benefits like deducting contributions or matching. Qualified education-related withdrawals from a 529 plan are not subject to federal income tax, and money in a 529 grows tax-free.

The way most people use a 529 plan is by putting in a small amount each year for 18 years, hoping there's growth along the way. Most people also use an allocation that gets more and more conservative as the targeted beneficiary gets closer to 18.

On the face of it, these are logical approaches: $5,000 or $10,000 a year adds up to plenty of tuition money after 18 years—and as the time to use that tuition money gets closer, it makes sense to reduce the risk.

However, it's important to take a step back and think about a 529 plan as an opportunity for multi-generational wealth transfer, rather than an opportunity to pay for one child's college expenses.

More and more people, like my clients Terry and Kelly, are choosing to over-fund a 529 plan with a significant one-time contribution. Terry and Kelly decided to contribute $100,000 to a 529 plan and put it 100% in stocks. Rather than changing the allocation to a more conservative balance over time, they plan to leave it 100% in stocks: the goal is not just for one child to use the

529 plan, but to have that child's children and their children's children use the money as well.

If you're able to over-fund a 529 plan like this, you're better off in the long term: you have a much larger initial figure that grows tax-free across a greater period. People are starting to look at the 529 plan as an opportunity not just to fund undergraduate expenses, but things like graduate school and education for grandchildren and great-grandchildren.

Over-funding a 529 plan creates an incredibly powerful multi-generational wealth transfer strategy—that, again, grows tax-free.

Strategy 7: Stockpile Your Losses

Tax loss harvesting is the final strategy we'll discuss in this chapter. It's used to offset gains in your taxable accounts. Tax loss harvesting does not work for 401(k) or IRA accounts, because they are already tax-sheltered. However, tax loss harvesting can be a great wealth maximizing tool for brokerage accounts.

Tax loss harvesting works like this: Say you have some securities that are underwater, and some that are gaining. You can sell the underwater securities at a loss, which then balances out the gains you made from selling other securities at a profit.

Put simply: you cancel out some of your gains with some of your losses, meaning you only pay taxes on the net profit.

Now, when you sell at a loss, you must make sure you replace those securities with something similar so that your portfolio's overall allocation remains the same. According to the IRS, however, you have to wait at least 30 days before purchasing any "substantially identical" securities, or your loss will not count towards tax loss harvesting.[62]

---

[62] Hayden, A. (2021).

Tax loss harvesting creates several benefits. It balances out capital gains, reduces your tax liability, and creates opportunities to continue maximizing your after-tax returns, since you can use money from the sale to balance and grow your portfolio.

Conclusions

Tax time doesn't have to be a stress-inducing season if you learn how to approach taxes from a strategic perspective. By focusing on maximizing your after-tax returns and engaging in tax planning rather than passive tax preparation, you'll be able to realize significant growth across your portfolios and develop a tax plan that supports a feeling of relaxed confidence in retirement.

Your taxes aren't the only financial area of your life that benefits from a good plan. In the next chapter, we're going to talk about building a planning habit.

Key Takeaways

- Too many of us take a passive approach to tax preparation when we should be taking an active approach to tax planning.

- The goal is not simply to avoid, minimize, or defer your tax burden. The goal of tax planning is to maximize your after-tax returns.

  o **Tax preparation:** The act of gathering the necessary information and paperwork to file your taxes or hand them off to an accountant. Tax preparation is tactical, backwards-looking, and obligatory.

- o **Tax planning:** Analysis of your financial situation coupled with a plan to ensure all elements work together to reduce your tax liability *and* maximize your wealth. Tax planning is strategic, forward-looking, and optional.

- It is more likely that taxes will increase than that they will decrease.

- Withdrawal sequencing is an important part of tax planning. The optimal sequence is:

  - o Taxable accounts first,
  - o Tax-deferred accounts second,
  - o Tax-exempt accounts last.

- A donor-advised fund allows you to avoid capital gains taxes on highly appreciated securities, claim a significant one-time tax deduction, and distribute money from the fund to 501(c)(3) organizations thereafter.

- The best time to establish a donor-advised fund is before you retire, when you're likely to be in a higher tax bracket.

- A 529 plan is a tax-advantaged investment account that can be used for qualified educational expenses.

- Tax loss harvesting allows you to offset gains by selling some securities at a loss.

11. Building Your Planning Habit

I'll never forget the first financial plan that I wrote, because I created it for my dad.

This was during my time at Stanford, when I was studying modern portfolio theory under Nobel Prize winner Bill Sharpe. One of our projects for Sharpe's class was to develop a financial plan. He wanted us to get some practical experience with the powerful financial concepts we were learning, and I decided to develop a plan for my dad.

Dad loved the plan, but he never got to use it. He died unexpectedly, a few weeks after I presented him with the plan I'd built. He was only 52 years old. My dad was never able to retire, or to put any of the aspects of that financial plan into practice.

I learned two key things from this tragic experience. First, I learned that I loved financial planning—and my dad's excitement about the plan I'd created for him showed I was good at it, too.

Second, and just as important, I learned that plans are great...but then life happens.

One and (Not) Done

Most financial plans, like the one I created for my dad, are one-time projects. I completed countless one-time projects during college, and I would go on to complete countless more in the early years of my career. I created many other one-and-done financial plans like the ones I'd learned how to make in school.

Most financial advisors, in fact, view a financial plan as a one-time engagement: You create the plan, then you enact the plan. Easy as that.

It seems like having a one-time financial plan should be enough to inspire a feeling of relaxed confidence: All you have to do is check your plan! However, the truth is that most one-time personal financial plans are marketing traps.

Personal financial planning was invented by life insurance agents as a marketing tactic to help them sell more life insurance policies. An agent will gather up a ton of information from you, then write up a financial plan that recommends you purchase a large, expensive life insurance policy—which they just so happen to provide! This still goes on all the time, unfortunately, and it's one of the reasons financial planning is an uncomfortable topic for many people.

In recent years, I've also seen the rise of another type of salesperson, who I call the asset gatherer. Many asset gatherers also use one-time financial plans to help them capture assets and convince the unwary to bring those assets under management—all so they can charge a 1% annual fee.

The problem with most one-time plans is that they ignore a simple but crucial fact: life *will* get in the way! A well-known military saying is that "No plan survives contact with the enemy."

While life isn't the enemy, it is certainly the case that no one-time plan will be able to withstand all the variables life throws at you. Having a singular financial plan can only give you a false sense of confidence, because when your plan is inevitably challenged by life, life *will* win.

One-time financial plans decay. They are simply not enough.

Planning as a Process

Before I began my career as a publisher for investment guidance company The Motley Fool, I spent six years in strategy consulting. I regularly wrote complex, detailed strategic plans that were over 50 pages long. Thanks to that work, I thought I understood the best ways to drive business strategy.

I was wrong.

Once I took on the role of publisher at The Motley Fool, we engaged a strategic consultant of our own. This consultant then presented us with a *one-page strategic plan*. At the time, this struck me as absolutely bizarre. Still, I tried to keep an open mind.

I quickly learned from the consultant that the purpose of limiting the plan to a single page was to dramatically decrease the plan's chances of decaying by making the document part of an ongoing process—and it worked!

The consultant introduced us to a new way of thinking about strategic planning, which involved having the management team update the one-page plan on a quarterly basis. That process would have been utterly impossible with the massive plans I'd created during my time as a strategy consultant. Having a one-page plan that we updated regularly gave us greater confidence in the plan, because we knew we would easily be able to adjust to new variables when they arose.

The one-page strategic plan reframed planning from one-and-done projects to an ongoing process, and I was hooked.

Projects vs. Processes

There are four main reasons to consider approaching your financial planning as an ongoing process, rather than a one-time project.

First, your portfolio changes. As discussed in Chapter Nine, your investment portfolio is unlikely to be the ideal perfect portfolio, and it will likely continue to change throughout your life.

You may decide to invest in a rental property at some point, using the building for vacation part of the time and renting it out at others. Your investing values and priorities may change.

If your financial plan doesn't reflect the ongoing changes in your portfolio, it will begin to decay.

Next, you change. Things in your life and in the lives of people you love change. Your health situation might alter as you age. Children and grandchildren will grow up and they might go to college, get married, start businesses, buy homes.

Your financial priorities may look very different five, 10, 15, or 20 years from now simply due to life changes, and your financial plan should be able to reflect those changes.

Second, your financial plan needs to be able to account for ongoing life changes, and it can't do that if it's a one-and-done project.

Third, things in the world change. Inflation might rise, taxes might go up, the stock market might take a serious tumble, and any number of other unforeseen world events could happen.

The COVID-19 pandemic introduced major changes in the world! If your financial plan is unchanging, then world events that affect the markets can simply break it.

If you make planning a process, you'll be able to adjust to new situations more easily.

Finally, there are financial activities that will occur every year in response to the above alterations. Making financial planning a process makes it easier to complete those activities and get back to focusing on your other goals and activities.

A one-and-done plan doesn't allow for the ongoing process of financial maintenance that everyone needs to perform.

Regarding your financial plan as one component of an ongoing process is a powerful shift, and it gives you more control over the plan and the outcomes you'll achieve.

However, there's one more step that you can take when thinking about a financial plan that inspires a feeling of relaxed confidence. As powerful as it is to approach financial planning as an ongoing process, it's even better to think about financial planning as a habit.

Building Your Planning Habit

Many processes can be automated; they happen in the background. Your financial plan isn't going to update itself every year, though. Your Roth Conversion won't convert itself, and your bond ladder won't climb the rungs on its own.

A powerful financial planning habit also supports the development of relaxed confidence in retirement. When your financial planning activities become automatic and habitual rather than reactive, you will find that you feel less anxious and far more confident and in control.

Working with a trustworthy financial advisor is another powerful way to increase your sense of relaxed confidence in retirement. While you'll want to be involved in keeping your financial plan up to date throughout the year, you can also relax in the knowledge that a reliable expert is also helping to keep you on track.

Turning your financial plan into a process that becomes a habit is essential.

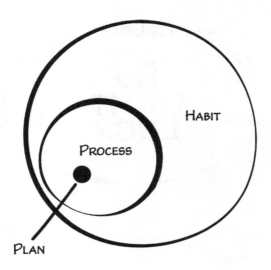

Habits are powerful and pervasive. William James called living creatures "bundles of habits,"[63] and habit researcher Wendy Wood found that a full 43% of our daily activities are habits we engage in, often without thinking about them![64]

It's much easier to make small course corrections on a habitual basis than it is to have to make a sudden dramatic shift because your one-and-done plan has failed.

You can think of a financial planning habit as a type of lane assist, which you might have in your car: As you start to drift away from the lane you want to be in, your planning habit will give you a gentle nudge back in the right direction.

Lane assist is much better for you, your passengers, and your car than having to suddenly jerk the wheel to avoid a collision!

Every habit is made up of three components: a trigger, a routine, and a reward.

The **trigger** is the signal that kicks off the routine. The trigger can be routine- or time-based, according to researchers.

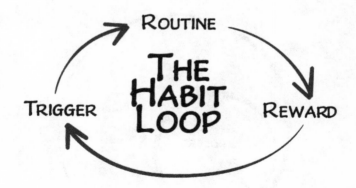

[63] James, W. (1890).

[64] Wood, W., Quinn, J. M., & Kashy, D. A. (2002).

For example, waking up and working out is a routine-based trigger: Your exercise follows another routine activity like waking up. Setting your alarm to remind you to work out at 6:00 a.m. is a time-based trigger, because you are cued to act at a particular time of day. Both methods are effective!

When it comes to your financial plan, the trigger might be a routine like the start of a new quarter, a time-based trigger like a scheduled meeting with your advisor, or another signal you design to remind you that it's time to engage in the habit.

The **routine** is the task or behavior itself. Exercising in the morning is a habit. Updating your financial plan and performing other necessary activities can become a habit.

The **reward** is how you benefit from the task or behavior. The reward might be the rush of endorphins you get from exercise or simply feeling better as you go about your day. When it comes to your financial planning habit, the reward is a feeling of relaxed confidence.

Personally, I have an afternoon latte habit. The trigger is finishing lunch—once I'm done eating, the craving kicks in and I start to recognize that it feels like it's the right time for that latte.

The routine involves heading to my usual coffee shop and ordering the latte, which I then drink as I go about my other afternoon habits. The reward, of course, is the feeling of energetic focus created by the caffeine.

Might I be better off without this habit? Maybe! But it is a very powerful one.

We all have countless habits, from when we brush our teeth to how and when we check email, and more. We can also build and change our habits in beneficial ways.

According to Wood's research, many people confuse habits and self-control.[65] A habit doesn't form because of self-discipline, but by repeating actions in a similar context across time and being rewarded

---

[65] Wood, W. (2019).

for completing the action.

Trigger, routine, reward—if you build the system, no superhuman self-control is required!

Forming a habit requires some initial effort, but once a habit is formed, we no longer need to think about it. As researchers like Dr. Phillippa Lally note, doing something for the first time requires planning and attention; habits are formed as we continue repeating an action in consistent settings over time.[66] Eventually, the action becomes efficient and automatic: It becomes a habit.

A financial planning habit is one of the most powerful habits we can form.

A Year in the Life

Let's consider what your planning habit might look like across a realistic time frame, such as a year.

The **trigger** for your planning habit could be as simple as a calendar reminder, letting you know that it's time to review the plan or meet with your advisor.

The **routines** are the financial tasks that you complete each year. Some tasks might be planning-oriented, while others might be more focused on implementation.

Even if you're working with a financial advisor who handles some of the tasks, you should at least be involved in the routines so you understand what's happening with your money.

The **reward** is the increased feeling of relaxed confidence in your financial life that will accompany completing each task—once it's done, you'll know your financial plan is on track, and you can relax.

If you want to add going out to dinner as a bit of an extra reward, that's fine too!

---

[66] Lally, P., van Jaarsveld, C. H. M., Potts, H. W. W., & Wardle, J. (2009).

When I first started working with Michael, he had a completely haphazard, ad hoc, and reactive approach to financial planning. The only real financial plan he had was preparing his taxes. Otherwise, he'd read something in the news, get worried about it, and start calling his friends to get their advice. The changes he made to his financial plan were always in reaction to something that had already happened.

Over a series of months and several meetings, we developed a set of financial planning habits instead. Now, years into our relationship, we have a clear and habitual cadence for annual financial planning activities.

Michael has a much greater sense of relaxed confidence in his financial life because he understands what the yearly calendar looks like. While no two years are the same, the habits provide structure, intention, and a forward-looking focus.

What follows is a sample list of routines that you might include in your own annual planning habits, organized by quarters.

These are the most common annual routines I see in my work with pre-retirees and retirees. The list is not comprehensive, but it should serve as a great starting point for thinking about your own financial planning habit.

First Quarter

- Revisit and update all financial goals, your cash flow worksheet, and your balance sheet.
- Review progress towards goals and modify your plan for the current year.
- Identify upcoming cash flow needs (episodic and ongoing).
- Execute a strategic rebalance.
- Gather tax documents and file tax returns.

Second Quarter

- Evaluate your investment risk profile, asset allocation, and rebalancing strategy.
- Evaluate your withdrawal strategy.
- Start current-year tax projections and evaluate projected income and withholdings.
- Evaluate and replenish your bond ladder and income floor.

Third Quarter

- Evaluate charitable goals and gift-giving strategy.
- Identify potential risks to the plan.
- Validate your risk management plan, including your protection plan against each risk.
- Evaluate and choose benefits or Medicare plans.

Fourth Quarter

- Evaluate your estate plan.
- Consider year-end tax planning strategies such as Roth conversions, tax loss harvesting, etc.
- Confirm account titles and beneficiaries.

Keep in mind that it takes time to form a new habit. The first couple of years of running these routines, whether alone or with an advisor, will take more effort. However, once the planning habit is well-established, it will all flow more easily.

Developing Your Planning Chops

Some people are natural planners, while others have to work at it a bit more. It turns out that brains play a role here. Natural planners have a brain structure and brain chemistry that make them adept at creating and following linear plans, while people with other types of brain structures and chemistry will struggle. However, there are ways to train yourself to become a good planner!

The Fishers, whom we met in Chapter Five, were on the cusp of retirement—but they hadn't yet done much planning and didn't feel they had great planning skills. They felt overwhelmed by everything they needed to accomplish to retire with confidence.

They needed to eat the elephant. That is, they needed to approach planning one bite at a time.

Through working together, we broke down all their retirement planning activities into small, achievable steps—analysis, action items, meetings, and so on. The Fishers couldn't adopt new habits until they first developed their planning chops.

Like everyone, they needed a custom set of routines that would work for them, ensuring their financial plans were enacted and that they had a clear sense of when we would meet and what we would do.

Time management coach Elizabeth Saunders takes several approaches to building planning skills with her clients, which are useful to consider when creating a financial planning habit.[67] These include:

- Recognizing your strengths and opportunities for growth. Saunders recommends the self-assessment in the book *Thriving in Mind* to help identify which part of your brain is dominant, and then using that awareness

---

[67] Saunders, E. G. (2017).

to help support your habits.[68]

- Accept that planning is challenging.[69] This is especially important if you are not a natural planner. If you treat planning like it "should be" easy when it's not, you're more likely to blame yourself, get frustrated, and give up. Instead, accept that planning and developing new habits are challenging activities, and prepare yourself to face difficulties.

- Don't engage in all-or-nothing thinking. Saunders points out that many people who struggle to plan also think their efforts are wasted if the plan didn't go perfectly.[70] Don't let the perfect be the enemy of the good! As discussed earlier in this chapter, all plans change when they come into contact with reality—having to adjust is not a sign of failure.

- Do what works for you.[71] Some people like lists. Other people prefer spreadsheets, personal productivity software, sticky notes, or handing off the whole system to a financial advisor. It's perfectly okay to try out different systems for planning until you find one that feels right for you.

- Don't give up.[72] As discussed in previous chapters, resilience is a priceless resource for your financial plan and your overall sense of relaxed confidence. The same is true when it comes to making financial planning a

---

[68] Ibid.
[69] Ibid.
[70] Ibid.
[71] Ibid.
[72] Ibid.

habit: if at first you don't succeed, cultivate the ability to try, try again.

- Rely on others. Saunders writes that working with people who *do* excel at planning can be incredibly helpful, as they might have suggestions or advice that comes in handy when you start to feel overwhelmed.[73] Finding the right helper is the subject of Chapter Thirteen, but for now just know that sometimes you will need to borrow someone else's brainpower.

Through strategies like these, the Fishers came to feel like they'd successfully eaten the elephant and were prepared to build the financial habits that create a sense of relaxed confidence. Not everyone is born with planning chops, but there are plenty of ways to develop a planning habit for your finances that works for your life.

Conclusions

Many of us are trained to think of financial planning as a one-and-done project, but our financial lives are simply more complex and changeable than that. Our portfolios and plans change, and the world is changing all the time.

Developing a flexible, resilient planning *habit* puts you in the driver's seat and gives you significantly more control over the outcome. We'll talk more about control in the next chapter.

---

[73] Ibid.

Key Takeaways

- Most financial plans are treated as one-and-done projects, but these decay and lose effectiveness over time.

- A financial planning process creates more flexibility and responsiveness. Processes:
    - Are responsive to changes in your portfolio.
    - Can account for changes in your life.
    - Enable you to adjust to new situations more quickly.
    - Align with the ongoing process of financial maintenance.

- The goal is to develop a financial planning *habit* that supports feelings of relaxed confidence in retirement.

- Every habit is made up of 3 components:
    - **Trigger:** The signal that kicks off the activity, e.g., finishing lunch.
    - **Routine:** The habitual activity itself, e.g., purchasing an afternoon latte.
    - **Reward:** The beneficial or pleasurable outcome of performing the habit, e.g., drinking the latte.

- Habits form by repeating actions in a similar context across time and being rewarded for completing the action.

- You can build a financial planning habit around tasks

that need to be performed every year, quarter, month, or week.

- You can learn planning skills even if you are not a natural planner:
    - o Recognize your strengths and opportunities for growth.
    - o Accept that planning is challenging.
    - o Don't engage in all-or-nothing thinking.
    - o Do what works for you.
    - o Don't give up.
    - o Rely on others.

12. The Conundrum of Control

As I mentioned back in Chapter Seven, I didn't have class on Wednesdays at Stanford, so I spent a lot of Tuesday afternoons and evenings in Vegas. In addition to learning the important difference between games of chance and games of skill at those blackjack and craps games, I also witnessed what I came to call the conundrum of control.

You win or lose at craps based on how the dice land. You have no influence over the roll, no matter how you shake the dice, how hard you blow on them, or whether you wore your lucky socks.

Yet I still watched people try, again and again, to exert some form of control through those rituals before each dice toss. Even though we know, rationally, that the result comes down to chance, people still felt compelled to try to control the outcome.

The conundrum of control is that there are outcomes we can control and outcomes we can't—and yet many of us spend enormous amounts of time focused on, and fretting about, what we *cannot* influence rather than what we *can*.

Your mindset regarding control has a significant impact on whether you're able to achieve a feeling of relaxed confidence in your retirement financial plan, and so the subject of this chapter is control.

You'll learn about the illusion of control, the locus of control, and how to deal with factors in life that are both within and outside of your control.

The Illusion of Control

Most of us believe that we have more control over the events of our lives than we actually do. Psychologist Ellen Langer called this the **illusion of control**.[74] The fancy dice tosses and good luck rituals at the craps table are all examples of how the illusion of control can shape our behavior.

The illusion of control also contributes to the planning fallacy. The planning fallacy occurs when we underestimate how long a future task will take—even when we already know that other, similar tasks tend to take longer than planned.

Think, for example, of a major construction project. How many times have you witnessed new construction that takes significantly longer and costs far more to complete than was originally projected? That's the planning fallacy at work.

The illusion of control contributes to the planning fallacy by leading us to assume we have more control over the project timeline than we truly do. The bias can cause us to fail to plan for pitfalls and problems, which then leads to delays, increased costs, and other issues.

NERDING OUT!

---

[74] Langer, E. J. (1975).

Additionally, while my friends and I had our fun in Vegas, excessive gambling is one way that the illusion of control can cause harm. Someone who believes they have control over the outcome of their dice throw is more likely to lose a significant amount of money than someone who accepts the roll as random and acknowledges they can't influence the result.

When it comes to the stock market, the illusion of control also has an effect. A 2010 study found that the more control traders feel they have over the outcome of their trades, the worse their performance is![75] The authors of the study concluded that, at least in trading, the illusion of control is a maladaptive trait.

Think about my clients Gavin and Kay, whom we met in Chapter Three. The illusion of control led Kay to feel as though she had more power over her employer's stock performance than she did—and that contributed to her dangerously concentrated position in a single stock.

The illusion of control can cause us to overlook risks and obstacles that should be taken seriously and can make it more challenging for us to recognize when it's time to call it quits. Gavin and Kay learned that lesson the hard way when their portfolio's value dropped by half, almost overnight.

However, while this cognitive bias might seem like a major barrier to developing a sense of relaxed confidence, the illusion of control—like optimism—can also be a good thing!

The illusion of control is the opposite of the cognitive bias called **learned helplessness**, a mental state associated with depression in which people who are faced with negative situations stop trying to improve things, because they feel that nothing they do will make a difference.[76] Learned helplessness primes people to give up, even when they could make a positive change.

The illusion of control, on the other hand, primes us to persist

---

[75] Fenton-O'Creevy, M., Nicholson, N., Soane, E., & Willman, P. (2010).
[76] Ackerman, C. E. (2021).

even when it might be more logical to give up.

One of the major benefits of the illusion of control is that it can prompt us to take responsibility when we're faced with a challenging situation. If we believe we have control over something, we're more likely to feel empowered to change or improve it, whether or not we can. Trying, however, always improves the odds of success.

The illusion of control is also associated with higher levels of optimism, with all the benefits of optimism discussed in Chapter Three. Feeling like you have a measure of control over the outcomes of your life—even if you don't, objectively speaking—contributes to a sense of mental well-being that leads to greater overall happiness.

The task is to develop a keen awareness of when the illusion of control is causing you to make risky decisions, and when it's helping you cultivate persistence and optimism. Part of this process involves identifying your own locus of control.

Where's Your Locus?

During the mid-twentieth century, psychologist Julian Rotter developed a concept he called the locus of control, which he explored in terms of the role of positive reinforcements or rewards.[77]

Rotter defined the **locus of control** as "the degree to which the individual perceives that the reward follows from, or is contingent upon, his behaviors or attributes versus the degree to which he feels the reward is controlled by forces outside himself."[78]

In more straightforward terms, your locus of control determines whether you think *you* have control over an outcome, or that control of the outcome exists *outside* of you.

Locus of control exists on a spectrum, with most of us feeling a stronger internal locus of control in some areas and a stronger external locus of control in others.

[77] Rotter, J. B. (1966).
[78] Ibid.

Contemporary research by Nichola Tyler, Roxanne Heffernan, and Clare-Ann Fortune builds on Rotter's original idea and shows that our locus of control develops based on associations and through reinforcement.[79]

- Your locus of control is internal if you believe you, or your internal characteristics, determine how things turn out.

- Your locus of control is external if you believe forces outside your control, like luck or fate or society, determine how things turn out.

NERDING OUT!

---

[79] Tyler, N., Heffernan, R., & Fortune, C-A. (2020).

The Control Conundrum

Identifying whether you have a strong internal or external locus of control can help you develop a better understanding of why you react to events in a particular way—and show you how shifting your locus of control might help.

There's also a decent argument to be made that being a bit further toward the internal locus end of the spectrum is better than tending toward the external locus side of things.

As with the illusion of control, having a strong internal locus of control can help you feel like you are able to shape outcomes in your life, leading to greater happiness, engagement, and persistence.

Take my client Wayne. When Wayne and his wife Janice came into my office, they were in their late 50s. Wayne had built a successful small business over 30 years and planned to sell it off. Then the COVID-19 pandemic started—and Wayne wound up getting a lot less out of the sale than he'd expected.

Wayne and Janice decided to retire anyway, but Wayne is still young and was feeling a bit nervous about how he'd pay bills for the rest of his life. He's antsy, and not the type of person to sit at home. He loves dealing with people and working on home improvement projects.

I worked with Wayne to help him examine some options based on his portfolio and his interests. After I helped him understand the economics of real estate portfolios, he ended up buying an investment property. Wayne quickly discovered that he loves owning real estate, being a landlord and property manager, working with his tenants, and fixing things up.

Not only that, but Wayne appreciates the greater sense of control a real estate investment gives him over his finances; he didn't just put all his cash into the stock market and sit back.

Instead, he was driven to explore an investment opportunity that allowed him to be more hands-on and entrepreneurial. The stable cash flow from the properties he works on gives Wayne a greater sense of relaxed confidence than the stock market would, and that's associated with Wayne's strong internal locus of control.

An internal locus of control is associated with a greater sense of responsibility for one's own actions, stronger feelings of self-efficacy, greater confidence in the face of challenges, and more. A stronger internal locus of control is similar in many ways to the growth mindset discussed in Chapter Three.

An external locus of control is associated with a focus on blaming external circumstances for failure, feeling a need to credit outside forces for success, and experiencing a sense of helplessness in the face of challenges. A stronger external locus of control is also akin to the fixed mindset discussed in Chapter Three.

Let's say your car breaks down unexpectedly, midway through a long drive. If you have a strong internal locus of control, you might feel a sense of chagrin for not having had the car looked at before you took off.

However, you're also more likely to feel like you're capable of handling the situation and to respond to the difficulty with confidence and equanimity: changing a flat tire yourself or figuring out who to call and getting the situation taken care of.

If you have a strong external locus of control, you might waste a bunch of time blaming the car manufacturer for not making a better car, complaining about the problem with your car, feeling the trip was ruined, and fretting about whether you will be able to solve the issue. A strong external locus of control makes the flat tire much more of a challenge than it really needs to be.

An internal locus of control equips you with many of the tools we've discussed for achieving a sense of relaxed confidence, and it's better for your life in general.

However, there's an important question that must be asked: Is a strong internal locus of control always better in your *financial* life?

Here are some mistakes I see people with a strong internal locus of control making when it comes to their finances.

Internals Take Their Own Predictions Seriously

We love to predict things. Human beings are addicted to predicting the future and paying attention to the predictions other people make—especially the negative ones, as we talked about in Chapter Three. In many aspects of our lives, predictions are useful: Weather and traffic reports are incredibly helpful, for example.

In investing, predictions can be an unmitigated disaster.

The stronger your internal locus of control, the more likely you are to believe that your predictions for your financial future will have an impact on the outcome.

You could easily convince yourself that spending 40 hours researching a company will help you make a better decision about its stock than researching it for 30 minutes. You could easily convince yourself that the biotech sector is undervalued, or that a certain investment manager is likely to outperform. You could convince yourself that you know it's time to get out of the stock market—or back in—and that your actions will shape the outcome in a meaningful way.

Yet think again of those traders and how feeling like they had control over the outcome of their trades worsened their performance!

If you have a strong internal locus of control, you're at risk of making all kinds of investing mistakes, like failing to adequately diversify, paying too much in investment expenses, trying to time the stock market, and so on.

Feeling like our attributes shape the outcome—even when they don't—primes us to make major investing errors.

Internals Can Fail to Plan

People with a strong internal locus of control tend to overestimate how much influence they have over the circumstances of their lives, especially in comparison to other people.

Maybe you're in great shape and you eat well, for example. While it's true that this reduces your risk of serious health problems, it doesn't eliminate them—but someone with a strong internal locus of control might fail to plan for what happens if they do get sick or injured. None of us can predict a car accident.

Maybe you've worked incredibly hard to become an expert in your career, and you've cultivated great relationships with your colleagues. Someone with a strong internal locus of control might attribute their career success entirely to those characteristics—and then get blindsided by being forced into an early retirement due to market forces outside their control.

A strong internal locus of control can keep us from thinking about risks that everyone faces when it comes to our financial lives. If you are more likely to think that your own actions determine the outcome, then you're less likely to plan for things like unexpected healthcare costs, downsizing at work, or economic downturns.

Because people with a strong internal locus of control feel like they have more influence over their lives than they do, they are at risk of failing to account for risk.

Internals Blame Themselves

People with a strong internal locus of control feel like they shape the outcome—and that's great when things are going well. When things go poorly, however, someone with a strong internal locus of control is more likely to feel self-doubt and to blame themselves for how things turned out.

If you have a strong internal locus of control and wind up with a serious health problem, you might blame yourself for it, even if the issue was entirely outside of your own control.

The same thing happens in finances. Someone with a strong internal locus of control might feel like a bad year for their portfolio is their fault and decide to make a bunch of changes to their portfolio to try to fix it, even though market performance is entirely outside of the control of any one individual.

Responding to external forces as though we can shape them can lead to investing mistakes and further self-doubt and self-blame.

Fortunately, it's possible to develop an awareness of your locus of control that allows you to make more rational decisions, and to reap the benefits of a strong internal locus of control while avoiding its pitfalls.

Being Two Places at Once

People who combine both internal and external loci of control are referred to as **bi-locals**.

Bi-local individuals tend to handle stress better than people with either strong internal or external loci of control, because they're able to take responsibility for what they can control while also acknowledging what they can't.

Put simply, your financial life needs to allow you to be in two places at once. You need to find a way to thread the needle between an internal and external locus of control.

LOCUS OF CONTROL

INTERNAL ⟵——————— BI-LOCAL ———————⟶ EXTERNAL

Becoming financially bi-local means identifying what you can control and taking responsibility for it, while also identifying what you can't control and letting go of it.

Working on developing a financially bi-local mindset is useful because it helps you cultivate the strengths associated with a strong internal locus of control and avoid the pitfalls of taking your own predictions seriously or failing to plan for risk.

Adopting a bi-local perspective also helps you see factors that are outside your control and acknowledge them as such—without feeling like you are nothing more than a victim of circumstance.

I'm convinced that, once we've identified our baseline locus of control, we should all strive to become financially bi-local.

What You Can't Control

When I was struggling with my confidence, I began to experience what's sometimes called anticipatory anxiety. Anticipatory anxiety caused me to ruminate about future events, even those that were unlikely to happen.

Ruminating on my fears of what *might* happen kept me focused on repetitive and negative thoughts that felt inescapable. I also struggled with catastrophic thinking, and always assumed that the worst outcome was the likeliest. For a long time, I felt like I was in a terrible situation that would only get worse.

Part of what kept me stuck in rumination was that I was focusing on things I could not control. Imagining the worst possible future and focusing on circumstances I had no impact on kept me from moving past my worries. I had a strong external locus of control, and it wasn't until I started shifting my perspective on topics like optimism and confidence that I was able to become more bi-local in my thinking.

It's important to recognize these risks and engage in a little bit of catastrophizing as you develop and maintain your financial plan. Imagine the worst that could happen, come up with a plan to minimize, mitigate, or transfer the risk and then, crucially, don't ruminate!

You can engage in catastrophic thinking about what you can't control when acting as your own chief risk officer—*but that's the only time you need to do it.* And, if you'd rather not do this type of catastrophic thinking, you can outsource it to a financial advisor.

It's important to recognize these risks and engage in a little bit of catastrophizing as you develop and maintain your financial plan.

Recognize what you can't control and be humble. Make a plan, and then trust the plan to do its job when and if a challenge arises.

One of my favorite strategies for developing a better bi-local outlook on life is cultivating greater mindfulness. I'll share one of my favorite exercises with you; this activity is perfect for helping you recognize what you can control, what you can't control, and where you might be tempted to ruminate or get stuck in bad feelings.

There are many things in life that you simply can't control, as we've discussed throughout the book:

- The stock market might collapse—really collapse.
- Inflation might surge.
- You might become embroiled in a lawsuit.
- You or a loved one might:
    - Experience health issues requiring long-term care.
    - Experience cognitive decline.
    - Die early.
    - Live much longer than you expect.

NERDING OUT!

Developing Mindfulness: Take a Ride on the Lazy River

If you find yourself worrying about things you can't control in your financial life, mindfulness techniques can help you bring your attention back to what you can control.

When I first started trying to change my ways of thinking, I found it difficult to believe that I could shift my attention and my thoughts away from my fears about what I couldn't control, but it is possible. It takes practice, and that practice pays off.

One exercise I have found helpful is called the Lazy River.[80] During this exercise, you pretend that you're on a lazy river, like the kind you might find at a water park.

Your thoughts, feelings, and physical sensations are all on this lazy river, each one in its own inner tube or raft, floating along. The goal of the exercise is to notice each of your thoughts, feelings, and sensations—without clinging to what you're noticing.

Just notice your thoughts, feelings, and sensations, and then let them float on by.

The Lazy River exercise is useful in a few ways. First, this type of mindfulness creates some separation between you and your thoughts. Thoughts, feelings, and sensations are fleeting. They come and they go, but we can decide whether and how deeply we want to engage with them.

Our thoughts, feelings, and sensations also don't have to dictate our actions and responses; we don't have to feel constantly reactive and trapped by our worries and fears. We can acknowledge them and let them go.

Through mindfulness activities like these, we can also learn how to focus on positive thoughts and emotions, as well as turn our attention to what we do have control over. This is a powerful exercise for cultivating a bi-local perspective and developing a greater sense of relaxed confidence.

---

[80] Burdick, D. (2021).

What You Can Control

As I rebuilt my confidence, learning about control, fixed vs. growth mindsets, and confidence and optimism helped me change my patterns of thinking. Instead of catastrophizing and ruminating about bad outcomes I couldn't control, I learned how to refocus my attention on what I *can* control.

When it comes to our financial lives, it's true that we don't have any impact on how the stock market performs or what the inflation rate is.

But there are plenty of things in your financial life that you clearly *do* have control over. We've touched on many of these in previous chapters, especially in the first section of the book.

You can control...

Factors like your values, your goals, and your mindset. For example:

- Naming your values and setting goals that are in alignment with those values.
- How you cultivate genuine confidence in your life.
- How you achieve a feeling of relaxed confidence.
- Your mindset, especially as it relates to optimism.
- Whether you have a growth mindset or a fixed mindset.

Getting crystal clear about your values, setting value-driven goals, and cultivating a growth mindset are all activities within your control. They're also activities that lead directly to feelings of relaxed confidence.

You can also control your behavior, especially around things like:

- The type of people you spend time with (optimists are recommended!).

- How much news you consume.
- Whether you focus on the negative or the positive.

There's a cliché that says you are the average of the five people you spend the most time with—so look at those people in your own life. Are they optimists? Do you feel happy around them, or do you leave feeling downcast and gloomy? The same questions apply when it comes to where you direct your attention. How much time do you spend reading the news (especially the financial news)? You have control here!

There are yet more areas where you have control, such as:

- Developing a planning habit, rather than treating your financial plan like a one-and-done project.

- Who you ask for help with your finances.

You can take the reins of financial planning, master some basic aspects of a planning habit, and enjoy the benefits. You get to decide who manages your finances, how much you want to pay, and how involved you want to be (we'll talk more about that in Chapter Thirteen).

While you can't control what the market does, you do have an extraordinary amount of control over your finances themselves. You get to decide what type of retirement you want to have, how much you want to spend, and when you want to retire.

Just look at this list! You have control over:

- The design and structure of an income floor that will meet your Needs for life.
- Deferring Social Security to increase your benefits.
- Whether you have a personal pension in the form of an income annuity.

- Whether you use a bond ladder.
- The diversification and shape of your investment portfolio.
- The amount of risk you are willing to bear.
- Having an investment portfolio that is built on skill and wealth management, rather than on luck.
- How much of your portfolio is devoted to Exploring.
- Your engagement with alternative investments, ESG investing, and investment properties.
- The strategies you choose to avoid, assume, mitigate, or transfer risks.
- Taking an active stance on tax planning and tax strategies that maximize your wealth.
- Employing an aggressive Roth Conversion strategy.
- Setting up your finances so you have the optimum withdrawal sequence.
- The asset location of everything in your portfolio.

When it comes to your financial planning for retirement and your mindset about finances and life, there are many, many things you *do* have control over!

Focusing your attention on what you can control will help you achieve a feeling of relaxed confidence.

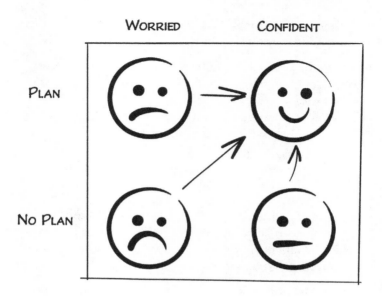

Conclusions

Rather than wasting time thinking about something you can't affect, you can increase your sense of self-efficacy by making the best possible choices in areas over which you do have control. Be humble about what you can't control and take responsibility for what you can.

In the next chapter, we'll take a look at what it means to share responsibility for your financial plan with an advisor—and why so many people are rightly skeptical of the financial advice industry.

Key Takeaways

- Your mindset regarding control has an impact on your ability to achieve a feeling of relaxed confidence in retirement.

- **Illusion of control:** The belief that we have more control over events in our lives than we do.

- **Locus of control:** Whether you think *you* have control over an outcome or think control over an outcome exists *outside* you.
    - A strong internal locus of control indicates you believe you determine outcomes.
    - A strong external locus of control indicates you believe outcomes are determined by forces outside you.

- In general, a stronger internal locus of control is preferable, because you are more likely to feel like you shape your life's direction, which leads to greater happiness, engagement, and persistence.

- **Bi-locals:** People who combine an internal and external locus of control. Bi-local individuals handle stress better because they can acknowledge what is within and outside of their control.

- There are many aspects of life that are outside our control. It's important to acknowledge and plan for them without ruminating.

- Cultivating mindful awareness of your thought patterns can help you avoid ruminating and feel more relaxed confidence.

- There are many aspects of life that are *within* our control, as well. These are the areas we should focus on!

13. Borrowing Brains

Asking for help is hard.

Those of us who are used to being high-achieving and self-reliant can find it especially hard to ask for help, because it means admitting we don't know everything already. It can feel like exposing a vulnerability, a weakness, or even a failure.

During the period when I'd lost my confidence, one of the things I struggled with was admitting that I could use a helping hand—asking for help felt like too much of a risk. However, I finally discovered professional and academic resources that made all the difference in rebuilding my confidence and getting me back to a productive, joyful life.

Over time, I learned that getting help doesn't mean I'm showcasing a huge flaw—instead, experts are sources of immense support and strength. Experts in the helping professions like researchers, doctors, nurses, teachers, and social workers are extremely well-trained, and they usually have people's best interests at heart.

As I read books on confidence and optimism and worked on cultivating a growth mindset, I emerged from my period of lost confidence with a renewed sense of profound gratitude for the helping professions.

I also found myself wishing that my own field—the field of financial advising—was considered a helping profession. I continue to be frustrated with the fact that it's just an industry.

I firmly believe that many people feel a deep sense of ambivalence about asking a financial advisor for help because we are not seen as helpers.

On the one hand, you probably already know that getting advice from a professional is wise. The stakes are high, and retirement planning is a complex undertaking.

On the other hand, asking for help is hard in general—and this is especially true when it comes to our money. No one wants to admit they don't understand something about their finances, even though retirement planning is a complex undertaking!

Further, you probably sense something is amiss in the financial advice industry, even if you can't quite put your finger on what it is.

Asking for help with your retirement financial plan can be an intimidating prospect in part because financial advising *is* an industry, rather than a helping profession. There are no guarantees that the advisor you find has your well-being at the core of their work like they would if they were a doctor. The first rule of financial advising is not, unfortunately, "Do no harm."

However, knowing when to ask for help and understanding how to find a true helper when it comes to your retirement financial plan is essential for providing you with a sense of relaxed confidence. After all, the entire goal of financial planning should be reducing stress and anxiety and promoting feelings of confidence.

In this chapter, we'll explore some of the conflicts that shape the financial advice industry as it currently stands. Then, we'll look at the three personality types that shape many people's approaches to financial planning: soloists, validators, and delegators. Finally, you'll learn how to identify a true helper.

Even if you realize that you're a committed soloist and you're pretty certain you don't want to work with an advisor, I encourage you to read the entirety of the chapter anyway. There are a lot of brains you can borrow without spending a dime on an advisor, and I'll show you how towards the end of the chapter.

The Financial Advice Industry

An industry produces and distributes things—those in industries are focused on their products and services and selling those products and services to their customers.

Think about a company like Apple: They want people to buy their laptops and phones. They design and market beautiful, functional products with all the bells and whistles included, because they want people to spend money on those items.

In contrast, consider the definition of a profession created by the Australian Council of Professions:

"A Profession is a disciplined group of individuals who adhere to ethical standards and who hold themselves out as and are accepted by the public as possessing special knowledge and skills in a widely recognized body of learning derived from research, education and training at a high level, and who are prepared to apply this knowledge and exercise these skills in the interest of others."[81]

A profession is not an industry. An industry is focused on distributing products; a profession is focused on knowledge, skills, and serving others.

This is why I say financial advising is an industry, not a helping profession:

Anyone can call themselves a financial advisor. The licensing hurdles are almost nonexistent, and many so-called financial advisors haven't mastered or researched anything beyond acquiring and maintaining client relationships. Most financial advisors are focused on sales—not on research, education, or even their clients' best interests.

On top of that, the prevailing compensation schemes across the industry don't promote high ethical standards, objectivity, or client well-being.

---

[81] What is a Profession?. (n.d.)

What's Missing

The financial advising industry is an industry because it lacks some of the key components of a profession, and especially of a helping profession. There are no widespread ethical standards in the industry that govern how to navigate conflicts of interest, which means that financial advisors are left to wrestle with their consciences or go numb to the conflicts they face.

On top of that, the industry lacks the mastery that comes from research and training, and those working in the industry are primed to apply what they do know to their own interests, rather than the interests of their clients.

What's missing is the wealth management equation introduced in Chapter Eight, where wealth management is the outcome of blending investment management and financial planning expertise in ways that keep your best interests at heart.

WEALTH MANAGEMENT = INVESTMENT MANAGEMENT + FINANCIAL PLANNING

Financial advising is not true wealth management because the prevailing methods of advisor compensation create significant conflicts of interest. Further, too few financial advisors demonstrate true mastery of the subject—and your portfolio can pay the price.

Fortunately, there are solutions to both problems that make it possible for you to ask for, and get, help that inspires true confidence. First, let's unpack exactly what the major problems are in the financial advising industry.

Problem 1: Advisor Compensation

There are two major figures in my industry that work within compensation schemes that create ethical conflicts of interest—I call them the Product Pusher and the Portfolio Pusher.

The Product Pusher

The Product Pusher is paid handsome—sometimes staggering—commissions for selling specific financial products to clients, whether or not those products are going to be in the clients' best long-term interests.

The Product Pusher's advice is geared toward selling the product, because that's what they are paid to do. There are, of course, Product Pushers who genuinely do want the best for their clients, but even these individuals are working under a troubling conflict of interest.

Product Pushers aren't paid to serve their clients' interests. They're paid to sell a product, and people tend to do what they get paid to do.

Additionally, a Product Pusher who's good at selling permanent life insurance and who really, truly believes in their product can be numbed to the conflict of interest they face each and every time they make a sale.

I know of a life insurance agent who sold a permanent life insurance policy that earned him a *$500,000 commission*. That policy may or may not have been the best way to accomplish the client's goals—but it was certainly the best way to earn the insurance agent a massive commission. And the client is, however indirectly, ultimately the one who winds up paying for that commission.

Even the most well-intentioned individual is likely to be biased toward a product that can net them a half a million dollars in a single sale, regardless of whether the product is the best solution for the client.

This conflict of interest is at the heart of all commission-based financial advising.

The Portfolio Pusher

The Portfolio Pusher works hard to gather all a client's assets into one place, and then charges a 1-2% management fee. There are two problems with this compensation model.

First, 1% doesn't sound like much to pay—but as we've already discussed in previous chapters, 1% of a big number is a big number. If your portfolio is $3 million, you'll be handing over $30,000 a year. A 1% fee is a massive drag on your portfolio and puts a major dent in your retirement spending abilities.

Recall from Chapter One that the 4% rule suggests $120,000 of annual spending from a $3 million portfolio. Do you really want to have only $90,000 available to spend because you have to fork over $30,000 to your advisor every year?

Second, like Product Pushers, Portfolio Pushers operate under troubling conflicts of interest. However, these conflicts can be more subtle than those faced by the Product Pusher.

Consider these common financial planning questions, which put a Portfolio Pusher into a hopeless bind:

- Should I take the monthly payments from my employer pension plan?

- Should I pay off my mortgage?

- Can I afford to buy a vacation home? Should I pay cash for it?

- Should I purchase an annuity to help power my income floor?

- Should I defer Social Security payments until I turn 70?

A Portfolio Pusher has a profound economic incentive answer "No" to each of these questions—even when it would be in the client's best interest to say yes.

Saying yes to any of these questions would result in a reduction in the size of the portfolio the Pusher is managing, which means their management fee gets correspondingly smaller.

Even the most well-meaning Portfolio Pusher will be faced with conflicts of interest like these, and in the end, their own bottom line might come out ahead of their clients' long-term well-being.

Objectivity and Compensation

We all know that most people respond to incentives, which is why the prevailing compensation schemes in the financial advice industry are such problems. I'll say it again: People tend to do what they get paid to do.

It's difficult, if not outright impossible, to make an objective decision if your decision-making capabilities are compromised by your pay structure.

Not only that, but the effects of these incentives can also be incredibly subtle. In other words, an otherwise honorable and upstanding person can be significantly influenced by the nature of their work and compensation—and not even recognize it! Compensation creates significant unconscious bias around conflicts of interest.

For example, one study found that setting compensation goals like end-of-year bonuses or rewards for hitting particular targets can increase managers' dishonesty and unethical behavior.[82]

As Bill Becker, one of the co-authors of the study, told ScienceDaily, "Goal fixation can have a profound impact on employee behavior," and that impact is often negative.[83]

In fact, the study found that it is the link between goals and financial incentives that is ultimately responsible for encouraging

---

[82] Sauer, S. J., Rodgers, M. S., Becker, W. J. (2018).
[83] Virginia Tech. (2018).

unethical behavior, and it even leads to worse treatment of clients![84]

Now consider the two most common compensation schemes in the financial industry: a commission-focused approach that creates financial incentives for Product Pushers, and a percentage-focused approach that creates financial incentives for Portfolio Pushers.

Is it any wonder that the financial advising industry has problems with objectivity?

The compensation schemes that result in Product and Portfolio Pushers currently dominate the financial advice industry, and neither one encourages objectivity or ethical treatment of clients.

A compensation scheme that introduces conflicts of interest cannot be objective; it will always be in service to someone else's bottom line.

The good news is that a small but growing percentage of firms and financial advisors is choosing compensation models that do promote objectivity, which frees advisors to focus on doing what's best for their clients.

A Better Way to Pay

There are ways to get the benefits of financial advising without dealing with the conflicts of interest that influence Product and Portfolio Pushers.

There is a small group of truly fixed flat fee financial advisors and firms. Under this model, you simply pay a fee for the financial advice. The fee is completely independent of the size of your portfolio, and the fee is the only way the advisor makes money.

This flat fee eliminates the conflicts of interest that crop up in both commission-based and percentage-based models and creates the possibility for the true mastery and objectivity clients need.

Under this setup, a financial advisor can have greater clarity of

---

[84] Sauer, S. J., Rodgers, M. S., Becker, W. J. (2018).

purpose. Their pay is the same regardless of the size of your portfolio, what products you buy, or how your assets are allocated—so the advisor can focus wholly on advice that is tailored to your unique situation and meets your specific needs.

A flat fee model is much more akin to the way someone in a true profession, like an accountant, charges their clients: There is a flat fee or an hourly rate that is the same across the board.

Now, admittedly, there are a few conflicts of interest that are inherent to any professional service fee structure.

Someone who charges a flat fee might still be inclined to make something simple sound more complex so that their clients feel dependent on them, use fear-based marketing tactics, make it seem like leaving the relationship is more complicated than it really is, or cut corners to drive up profits.

Every business has multiple constituents, from the owner and potential shareholders to the employees to the clients. There is no business model that doesn't have some conflicts of interest because money is changing hands.

However, I would argue the flat fee model is still the model that is most likely to connect you with a professional who can be objective about your portfolio, and who is incentivized to develop true mastery of wealth management—not just good sales skills.

When it comes to your own retirement planning and financial needs, I would urge you to seek out a financial advisor who charges a flat fee.

By doing so, you'll avoid the conflicts of interest presented by Product and Portfolio Pushers and you'll work with an advisor who is more likely to have the objectivity to put your best interests at the heart of their advice.

The Devil You Know

Many people who come into my office feel incredibly ambivalent about their current financial advisors.

On the one hand, people like my client Terri tend to be exceptionally well-educated and understand that paying a 1% fee is like acid dripping on your portfolio—you might not see the damage right away, but after 30 or 40 years, that acid will corrode and ultimately devastate your finances.

On the other hand, many financial advisors are expert relationship managers. Terri, for example, is a CalTech-educated senior professional. She knew that paying $60,000 a year simply for portfolio management was a bad deal. Yet she stayed with a firm that charged a 1% fee for 10 years past the point where she'd come to question it.

Why? Because she knew the people there. She knew how to read the statements. She felt a connection to the financial planner who oversaw her account, a person who took pains to build that connection. It's hard to break off a relationship—even a professional, service-based relationship—because most people don't want to deliver bad news.

However, Terri eventually got to a point where she knew that she couldn't continue to justify the cost to her portfolio, and she discovered that the process of "breaking up" with her firm wasn't as painful as she'd imagined.

First, your advisor doesn't need to do anything when you decide to make a change. You don't need to contact them, get their permission, or have them fill out any paperwork. You'll simply authorize the new firm to transfer the assets in kind (to avoid creating a taxable event).

Second, when you do decide to let your former firm know you've moved on, it's important to remember that this is a service-based transactional relationship. Circumstances change, and it's not personal: this decision is about you, your family, and the right model for your finances in the long-term. All you're doing is making sure your list of service providers is useful to you.

Ideally, that new service provider will also have mastered financial planning!

Problem 2: Mastery

Dr. Anders Ericsson[85] first proposed the idea that mastery requires 10,000 hours of practice, which was popularized by Malcolm Gladwell.[86] While Ericsson has critiqued the way the 10,000-hour rule is applied, the fact remains that significant effort must be expended in the pursuit of true mastery.[87]

Whether or not a full 10,000 hours of practice is the standard, most financial advisors fall woefully short, especially when it comes to the content of financial planning and investment management.

What the most successful financial advisors *have* mastered are the skills of acquiring clients, selling products, and gathering assets. These skills are critical for building financial advisory businesses, but they have nothing to do with driving good financial outcomes for clients.

Some financial advisors have studied extensively and have robust skills in true financial planning. These true planning experts come in two flavors: Generalists and Specialists.

Generalists

Generalist planning experts are Certified Financial Planners who serve a wide variety of clients: younger clients and older clients, those from the middle class, as well as the wildly affluent.

A generalist has both deep and broad knowledge of financial planning and focuses on generating actual benefits for their clients—not serving their own bottom line.

If you're more than five years from retirement, a generalist planning expert would be a great person to work with.

---

[85] Young, J. R. (2020).
[86] Gladwell, M. (2008).
[87] Good Life Project. (2020).

Specialists

Specialist planning experts are certified financial planners who serve people in a specific niche: new parents, women, executives, doctors, pre-retirees, and retirees.

A specialist has deep knowledge of the financial needs of those in the niche they serve and will customize the financial plans they develop around those needs.

If you're within five years of retiring or are already retired, a specialist planning expert focused on retirement planning is the type of help you should seek. There are individual financial planners and firms that specialize in all the issues facing pre-retirees and retirees.

Retirement income planning is a lot more complex than wealth-building, and it's essential to find an expert in it. In addition to finding a certified financial planner, find a firm that has individuals on staff with the Retirement Income Certified Professional (RICP) designation.

Soloists, Validators, and Delegators— Oh My!

Now that you know the major problems of the financial advising industry and how to better identify the type of helper who can help you, it's useful to have a framework for understanding your own approach to financial planning.

Once you know what your financial planning personality type is, you can pursue the level of help that best matches it and understand how to feel confident in the help you've chosen.

Soloists

Soloists or DIYers, as you might guess from the name, are people who prefer to be fully in charge of their own financial planning.[88]

A soloist is likely comfortable taking a DIY approach to their financial plan, figuring out all the details alone or with their partner. Soloists typically don't feel like they need any outside help.

You might be a soloist if you:

- Already feel confident in your financial plan.

- Prefer to have complete insight into and control over every aspect of your financial plan.

- Resist being "told what to do."

The biggest benefit of being a soloist is, of course, that it's free. You evade all the conflicts of interest associated with the financial advice industry, and you don't pay any fees even to a flat fee advisor. A soloist has complete control over every aspect of their plan.

The downside of being a soloist is that ignorance is *not* bliss when it comes to financial planning. Mistakes you make when going it alone can be devastating to your retirement finances, and a skilled advisor is likely to know strategies for financial planning that even the most interested soloist hasn't encountered.

Validators

Validators are individuals who may have already created a financial plan on their own, or who feel confident in doing so, but

---

[88] Stich, A. (2020).

who also value independent feedback from an expert source.[89]

A validator is not going to take a full DIY approach when it comes to their financial plan but may create a plan on their own and then solicit input from advisors. Validators might also work collaboratively with an advisor to create a plan, and then check back in with that advisor periodically.

You might be a validator if you:

- Are confident in your financial plan but want to have your plan checked over by a professional.

- Prefer to have most of the control over your financial plan and appreciate outside insights.

- Enjoy a collaborative approach to important projects like retirement planning.

There are numerous benefits to being a validator or shifting from a soloist approach to a validator stance. A validator still has primary responsibility for their financial plan—but is likely to save significant time and money on developing it.

Working with a trustworthy financial advisor to validate the plan also increases the odds that you will be able to make use of financial planning software and strategies that help your portfolio grow.

Being a validator does require some investment of time and money on your part, but the return on investment often more than compensates for it.

---

[89] Ibid.

Delegators

Delegators are those who want their financial advisor to take the reins when it comes to financial planning.[90] They may not feel confident about generating a financial plan themselves or might want to have a more hands-off approach.

You might be a delegator if you:

- Aren't totally confident in your financial plan and feel you need expert insight.

- Prefer to hand off your financial plan to an advisor and only check in on it periodically.

- Want someone else to take the lead on designing and implementing your retirement financial plan.

A delegator benefits from being able to fully hand off the retirement financial plan to an expert—while you will invest some money in the advisor's expertise, you save the time and headaches of doing all the work yourself.

Delegators are likely to have less in-depth insight into their financial plan than soloists or validators, and many delegators prefer to focus their energy and attention on other parts of their lives.

You may find that your financial personality type changes depending on your goals and your current stage of life.

During your wealth accumulation years, for example, you may be more of a soloist. When the goal is simply to live below your means and grow your money, taking a DIY approach to financial planning isn't all that hard.

As people approach retirement, however, the validator and

---

[90] Ibid.

delegator stances often become more attractive. Many people discover that retirement planning—figuring out how to spend the wealth they've built—is far more complex and high-stakes than building it.

Getting expert insight and support as you build and refine your plan can increase your feelings of relaxed confidence. Shifting from a soloist to a validator perspective as you approach your retirement years can help you cultivate a feeling of relaxed confidence through active engagement with your planning habit combined with the knowledge and expertise of a financial advisor.

My client Dean, for example, was a soloist for most of his life. When we met, he'd read more about investment and financial planning than I had, and he came to every meeting guns blazing, ready with white papers and sharp questions. I loved it!

Dean was interested in getting help with his financial plan but didn't want to transfer his assets right away. While "percentage advisors" require you to transfer your assets to kick off the relationship, our firm's flat fee model gives our new clients more flexibility. I could meet Dean where he was at, answer his questions, and show him the simulations and calculations behind every one of our recommendations.

While Dean will never be a delegator—he's too interested in finances to fully hand things off to me—he did complete the transition from soloist to validator, eventually passing us his entire life savings to manage. The open dialogue, transparency, and conversations we had about exactly why I made my recommendations helped Dean gain confidence and feel more relaxed about accepting outside help as he approached the high-stakes financial decisions around retirement.

Once you're close to or in retirement, you may also find that the trade-off between time and money means becoming a validator or delegator best fits your lifestyle. Gaining extra time with your loved ones, traveling more, and worrying less because you hand off some or all your financial planning to an expert can be worth far more than what you pay your advisor.

Whatever your planning personality type happens to be, it's

essential to know how to find help that you can rely on. Validators and delegators need to be certain they can trust the financial advisor they choose to work with.

Being Confident in Your Helper

Navigating conflicts of interest with your financial advisor is unlikely to inspire feelings of relaxed confidence. It's the underlying awareness of the Product and Portfolio Pushers' inherent conflicts of interest that makes many people feel ambivalent about asking for help with their finances in the first place.

It is exponentially harder to seek assistance if you feel like you can't fully trust the person you're working with.

The goal of all financial planning activities should be to help you achieve and maintain the feeling of relaxed confidence in your finance for the rest of your life. Remember that confidence comes from the Latin word for trust, and trust should be driven by credibility.

Mastery and objectivity drive trust, and trust drives confidence. Without mastery and objectivity, you are left with nothing—or, worse, you're left with a sense of false confidence.

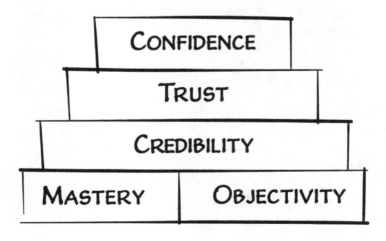

When it comes to asking for help, find someone who has mastered retirement income planning, and who is free to be objective because they charge a fixed flat fee for their services.

For the DIY Crowd

Even soloists can use a helping hand now and again, and there are ways for even the most die-hard DIYer to get help without hiring a financial advisor.

If you are committed to tackling the creation, implementation, and maintenance of your retirement financial plan on your own, there are several brains I highly recommend you borrow:

- Wade Pfau of Retirement Researcher, for his work on income annuities as an essential part of your Income Floor

- Harry Markowitz, the father of Modern Portfolio Theory, for understanding the power of diversification

- Jack Bogle, the founder of Vanguard, for creating the first index fund and low-fee index fund investing

- Fama and French, professors who developed the Fama-French three-factor model for describing stock returns

- Peter Bernstein, the financial historian and economist who developed the efficient-market hypothesis

- Daniel Kahneman, psychologist and Nobel Prize-winning economist who has written books like *Thinking, Fast and Slow* and *Noise: A Flaw in Human Judgment*

- Carol Dweck, for her psychological work on mindset and cultivating a growth mindset in particular

- Martin Seligman, for his books like *Learned Optimism* and *Authentic Happiness*

- Charles Duhigg, for his work on habit, including books like *The Power of Habit* and *Smarter Faster Better*

Conclusions

Getting help with your retirement planning habit can make a huge difference for your finances. However, the conflicts of interest present in the prevailing compensation schemes in the financial advice industry and the lack of mastery among many advisors make it difficult to find a helper you can rely on with true confidence.

Objectivity and mastery are key drivers of trust and confidence, and flat fee advisors can provide both. After reading this chapter, you are equipped with the information you need to ask for—and receive—help that truly centers your financial well-being.

Key Takeaways

- The financial advising industry is an industry rather than a helping profession.
  - **Profession:** A discipline with ethical standards, special knowledge and skills, research-driven training and practices, and an emphasis on the greater good.

- Anyone can call themselves a financial advisor. Most financial advisors lack objectivity and mastery, and the prevailing industry compensation schemes create ethical conflicts of interest.
  - **Product Pushers:** Commissioned advisors whose income depends on selling you lucrative (for them) products and services.

- o **Portfolio Pushers:** Advisors whose income depends on capturing your assets, holding on to them tightly, and charging you 1% (or so) every year.

- **Flat Fee Advisors:** Wealth managers who charge a fixed flat rate regardless of a client's portfolio size or what products are selected. Flat fee advising avoids the conflicts of interest associated with Product and Portfolio Pushers and creates room for objectivity and mastery.

- **Generalist Advisors** work with a wide variety of clients and are a good option if you are 5+ years from retirement. **Specialist Advisors** work with a specific client niche. Pre-retirees and retirees should seek out a Retirement Income Certified Professional (RICP).

- Each of us falls into one segment of "self-directedness:"
  - o **Soloists:** People who prefer to be fully in charge of their money (strategy and execution).
  - o **Validators:** People who value expert input and collaboration on their retirement financial plans.
  - o **Delegators:** People who prefer to hand off their entire retirement financial plan to an expert.

- Many soloists become validators as they face the time-consuming and potentially expensive risks of financial planning.

- The goal of all financial planning activities should be achieving and maintaining a feeling of relaxed confidence.

14. Be the Bird

A bird sitting on a tree is never afraid of the branch breaking, because its trust is not on the branch but on its own wings.

—Charlie Wardle

We covered a lot of ground today. We talked about you and we talked about me, too. You met a few of my mentors, some of my clients at my life's work, Clark Asset Management, and heard a little about my firm's approach to wealth management.

We talked a *lot* about birds—which sounds goofy, even to me.

Remember, I'm a math nerd. My colleagues once called me a robot! Ten years ago, if something couldn't be modeled, tracked in a spreadsheet, or at bare minimum, quantified, it might as well have not existed.

Like everything in my life, managing my wealth and planning my own retirement was a theoretical, even a mathematical, exercise. Ten years ago, this book would have had far fewer people, zero birds, and many more Greek letters.

But don't get the wrong idea. Math and theory are important. None of the concepts and strategies we discussed in this book would have been possible without them. Nor would I have had the language to share them with you.

And I don't just mean concepts like Sharpe ratios and bond durations. Even such kitchen-table, seemingly tactical concepts as safe withdrawal rates, tax diversification, asset "location," and income floors are in some sense "math."

The process of setting long-term financial goals requires some level of abstraction and quantification. Yet, for all that, "theory" and "running the numbers" are only part of the process I wanted to share with you—and, in my view, a small part.

I'm not exaggerating when I say it took me years to realize this. My guess is that it comes easier to you. But what is this other—again, I'd argue, most vital—part of the retirement planning process? You probably guessed that one, too.

Of course, I mean the human element.

I know that might sound a little "new age," but I'm serious. It's why I so painstakingly built out my team of professionals at my firm. It's also why we are so careful when taking on new clients. It's why, to this day, I insist on learning about every client we take on so that I can contribute to their strategies and well-being.

It's also why, while I strongly recommend and sincerely hope that you will keep this book on hand as a reference, even an instruction manual of sorts, for now: I want you to forget the math.

If you take away just two points from our conversation today, I hope they're the following. First, I encourage you to do everything in your power to adopt and cultivate a planning habit, as we discussed in Chapter Eleven, whether this means working on your own or with a trusted advisor.*

---

*It's true. If you are a soloist, as discussed in Chapter Thirteen, or have had the good fortune of hooking up with an advisor you trust, our work is done. If you're not sure, take a moment to read the "unofficial" chapter just ahead, revealing how I approach the subject with potential clients. If nothing else, it will help you know what to look for should the time come when you, like so many smart and capable people I meet with, consider a transition to the role of validator or even delegator.

Remember, among other benefits, approaching financial planning as a lifelong process allows you to more readily respond to new situations, including changes in your portfolio, the world writ large, and your personal life—which, in turn, leads directly to the sense of relaxed confidence we've been searching for.

Second, I hope you will do your best to foster an attitude of gratitude and optimism, as discussed in Chapter Three. This may come easier to you than it did to me, especially if you were fortunate to have been born with a sunny disposition and a growth mindset. If not, I encourage you to give it a try.

Not only does optimism allow us to place our trust in, and hitch a ride on, the unprecedented wealth-building engine of capitalism, it just makes us happier people. Moreover, it is fundamental to developing the deep feeling of relaxed confidence that is, again, my ultimate goal for you.

If you can promise me those two things, everything else will more or less fall into place—whether you decide to go it alone or choose to work with a professional advisor.

Income streams, investment selection, portfolio construction, tax and estate management—the rest is all details. Important, sometimes baffling and potentially life-changing details, but details nonetheless.

Surprised? Imagine how I feel!

I spent thousands of hours studying and reading and training and, yes, testing to gain the expertise and credentials to put together my advisory firm and confidently help you manage your wealth and plan your retirement...

All so I could tell you to "plan and be happy?" I get it. Like most everything in this book, it sounds unconventional, but here we are.

So, are you ready? Great. You've got everything you need. You can do this.

Let's be the bird.

From the Desk of Bradley Clark: What to Do Now

If you scan the mainstream financial news sites as I do, you've probably come across a reader Q&A that goes something like this:

> *Dear Guru: My financial advisor bills me like clockwork, $20,000 (or $30,000 or $40,000) each year. Yet he invests my money entirely in index funds. If we're not even trying to beat the market, isn't this something I could do myself FOR FREE?"*

At first blush, this sounds like an investing question or a gripe about cost. But I think it's something else. I'll let you mull it over. Then I'll tell you what I think the reader's really getting at.

But first things first. Since you volunteered to plow on through this letter, I'm going to make a few assumptions. First, I'm going to assume that you either...

1. Don't currently work with an advisor and are considering a transition from DIY to a less burdensome role of validator or even delegator. Or...

2. You have worked with an advisor but are not entirely satisfied with what you're getting out of the relationship—and you're open to considering a change.

I'll also assume you grasp the magnitude of everything we discussed in this book and are serious about getting this right. If any of these situations sounds like you, here's what I suggest.

Rather than bore you further by telling you "what to expect" or "what to look out for," how about I instead *show you* exactly how I approach a prospective new client at my firm?

This way, you can decide for yourself whether your current advisor could be doing better. Likewise, you'll get a better sense of what you should expect from a prospective advisor should the conversation arise in the future (plus one more intriguing alternative that we'll discuss in just a moment).

For the sake of argument, let's imagine you've successfully managed your own saving, investing, and planning for years. Yet, more and more, you...

1. Worry about whether your portfolio is truly positioned to provide the wealth and stable, predictable income you need right now—or will need once you retire...

2. Find yourself losing sleep and fretting over your investments and your nest egg, especially given the recent economic turmoil and market volatility...

3. Suspect you're ready to pass the reins and focus on your family, your hobbies, or other matters.

Or maybe you've been working with an advisor, but recently experienced a surprise windfall or life change, either at home or at work. Maybe your long-term plans or needs have simply gotten more, let's say, complicated... As we discussed in the book, the accumulation phase of life is straightforward, even easy. Decumulation? That's a whole other story.

Or maybe you're just not getting the attention and expertise you feel you deserve. I could go on, but I think you get it. Whatever the reason, let's imagine you and I have set a time to chat.

Great!

Almost certainly we'll meet because you listened to a podcast I was on, watched one of my video tutorials, or read my online content. Either that, or you found me through a website that shares my disdain for the financial advising industry's status quo.

(If you haven't seen my videos or my online course, *10 Easy Steps to Retirement Income for Life*, I'll show you how to check them out just below. Don't worry, I won't ask for anything in return.)

I say "almost certainly" because we don't spend our time and energy soliciting new business. In fact, my planners don't work the phones, attend networking luncheons, or annoy their family and friends. They're simply not responsible for building a clientele or, even more problematic, capturing assets.

Not only does this allow us to focus 100% on assessing and meeting our clients' needs, it means we work only with clients where the "fit" is perfect. Frankly, you might be surprised by how much time traditional advisors spend trying to "build their book."

(Which is not to say you can't get decent service from a planner or advisor whose livelihood depends on attracting new clients and capturing assets. But the arrangement does present a conflict of interest worth considering, as covered in Chapter Thirteen.)

In any event, distracted advisors, misaligned incentives, and compensation conflicts are no longer your concern. One way or another, you found your way to us (perhaps through reading this book right now!).

So let's walk through what could happen next...

First, we'll have a short meeting, maybe 20 or 30 minutes max, either over video or an old-school phone call. This first meeting has one and only one goal: to determine our mutual compatibility. Or, to be even more blunt, to determine whether a second meeting is in order.

That's it. But it is critical—and I hope it doesn't make you uncomfortable. In this introductory meeting, we really are screening each other. It's crucial to me that we work only with clients where the fit is just right, just as I imagine it is to you.

This is our first win-win! Assuming all goes well...

We'll schedule a second call. This one might be 30 to 45 minutes, or longer if you like. The second call will also happen by phone or by video, though we can meet in person if you prefer (and assuming you're located near one of my senior planners). It's entirely up to you.

On this call, we'll get down to the nuts and bolts of our service, our revolutionary "one-flat-fee-for-all" structure, and what's involved in bringing you on board. Equally important, you'll hear more about my team—including what you can expect from us day-to-day, month-to-month, and year-to-year.

Now, here's what we probably won't discuss…

We won't fret over on how big or small your investment portfolio is. We won't discuss how quickly we can get your assets transferred to the firm. Nor will we go over what kind of returns you are currently getting or can expect to get from your investments should you sign on as a client.

Most important, you won't hear a lot of dire warnings or outlandish promises. There will be no pressure. Instead, we'll talk more deeply about you: your concerns, your beliefs, what's going on in your life, and perhaps above all, your goals.

We will, however, contrast what you can expect to pay for our services with what you would pay under a traditional asset capture model based on the size of your portfolio. No exaggeration, lifetime savings could exceed $1 million for many of our clients.

Once we've both decided to proceed, the real fun begins. Over the next three months (three or four meetings in all), we'll undertake the process of bringing you formally into the Clark Asset Management family.

This process culminates in the gradual repositioning of your assets into superior, low-cost investments that will power the truly custom financial plan my senior planners and I will have built exclusively for you.

Among other technicalities, this might include designing and custom building an income floor, like the one we talked about in

Chapter Six, to fund your daily spending (this is just one of many benefits of our specific retirement income expertise that's not offered by typical financial advisors). We'll also assess the risks you face in retirement and decide how to approach those risks, and more.

Yet, even that's just the beginning…

Going forward, once you've signed off and we've put your plan in place, my team and I will constantly monitor and massage the plan, relying on the concepts and principles we'll discuss at length during the onboarding process and that you read about in this book.

How often will we chat? Well, that's up to you. You can be as hands-on or hands-off as you like. Remember, we're here to make your life easier. But you can rest assured that, at bare minimum, you can expect two calls each year, and that we'll always be here for you whenever you want to talk.

Of course, there's much more I won't go into here. But in my humble opinion, this is the very least you should expect from me— or for that matter, any reputable financial planner or advisor you do business with.

Which brings us back to the reader question we addressed up top. You remember, the one about mediocre investment returns, index funds, and unfair advisor fees. Did you guess what the inquiry really is about?

Well, here's what I think…

I don't believe this is a question about investment returns or management fees at all. In my view, it's a screaming red flag that the reader is not receiving any or all of the services we just discussed— and that you should demand of a true wealth advisor.

Including, but not limited to, the delivery of…

1. A living, breathing, dynamic financial plan that is custom-built for you and aligns your specific goals and needs with your diversified, balanced investment portfolio...

2. Constant monitoring and regular updating that reflects any subsequent life events—including changes in your personal Needs, Wants, and Wishes...

3. Optimization that manages your most pressing financial risks and assures a minimal tax burden over the course of your accumulation and decumulation life phases.

And, perhaps most important of all, full transparency and regular, scheduled communication, PLUS easy, friendly, unlimited access to your senior planner and staff any time a question should arise, no matter how "small."

Namely, the very benefits we promise to each and every client we take on at Clark Asset Management. Remember the wealth management equation we talked about:

And remember this, too...

You should never mistake your wealth advisor for a stock-picker or, best case, a mere portfolio manager.

Nor should you be handed a one-off, static, one-time plan and contacted only for the purpose of quarterly billing!

More than anything, you should never be left in the dark, wondering what your advisor is doing and what *exactly* it is you're paying them for.

Not only is this ineffective (and surprisingly common), it's a major driver of distrust in the financial services industry. It's also what we are trying to disrupt at Clark Asset Management.

So there you have it. If any of this sounds good to you, I encourage you to take a minute to go to BradleyClark.com and bookmark the site so you'll have it on hand when you need it.

You'll get instant free access to my course, *10 Steps to Retirement Income for Life,* along with my blog and other resources, where I've distilled everything I learned in two decades in the financial services industry. I think you'll find it's a perfect complement to everything we discussed today.

More important, you can schedule a call with one of my senior planners or with me personally. We'd be happy to answer any questions you might have, whether they're about the concepts in this book or what we might be able to do for you personally, in the real world.

Of course, there is no cost or obligation on your part. And I guarantee you there will be no selling or pressure of any kind whatsoever. Just valuable information and a straightforward, friendly conversation…

www.BradleyClark.com

Check it out right now and thanks for reading. I'll see you there!

Brad Clark, CFP©, RICP©

P.S. You can book a call with one of my planners through my website. But, as a personal thank you for reading my book, I'd like to offer you a call with me directly. You can schedule your call at:

BradleyClark.com/bookbonus

Acknowledgments

Developing a solid wealth management plan is a lot like writing a book: it's easier when you have a planning habit and some support. This book started with one of my big ideas and spiraled out from there, pulling in many collaborators.

My sincere thanks to my friend and Foolish colleague, Paul Elliott. Your sharp commentary and wordsmithing took the writing to a new level.

Thanks are also owed to Marina Lohse, Positive Psychology Coach, and Eloise Russo, Executive Coach, for reading an early version of the manuscript and meeting with me to offer your feedback on research in psychology, the benefits of optimism, and more. Your insights shaped and improved the text in innumerable ways.

To my beta readers—Zubia Abbasi, Kyra Byrne, Sue Campbell, Spencer Downing, Paul Elliott, Justin Estes, Michael Fechter, Jon Gove, Ryan Healy, Tom Holbrook, Marina Lohse, Eloise Russo, Benji Seyler, Mark Shields, Matt Smith, David Sylvester, Todd Thompson, and Rick Wolff—thank you, thank you, thank you. Your feedback was invaluable. Your insights helped me totally reimagine the message of the book and the impact it could have on readers. This book is what it is in large part because of you.

Benji Seyler—the book wouldn't be the same without your help in recreating my whiteboard evangelism in illustrated form. The illustrations throughout the book are exactly what it needed. And that cover! I needed something that would make a statement, and you went above and beyond. Thank you for everything.

Thank you to my college singing buddy Larry Finer for "nerding out" and writing the "inclusion-exclusion" code to compute the probabilities of different numbers of risks in retirement.

Bailey Lang, you've been an essential contributor from the very beginning of this process as both developmental editor and project manager. This book simply wouldn't exist without your feedback, insights, and keen input.

To Tom Holbrook and team at Piscataqua Press—thank you for all of your support in getting this passion project designed, published, and in the hands of readers.

To my team at Clark Asset Management, thank you, from the bottom of my heart, for the work you put in every single day to serve our clients and turn the financial advice industry into a helping profession.

Thanks to my dear (and old) friends Jon, Jack, Mark, and Jordan, for supporting me when I set off to build my firm.

To all our clients, whom we are truly honored to serve. Thank you for your trust and everything you teach us every day.

To my family and friends, thank you for always believing in me, and for your unwavering support.

References

AARP NRTA. (n. d.) The importance of your pension. NRTA Pension Education Toolkit. https://assets.aarp.org/www.aarp.org_/articles/work/importance-of-pension-non-ss-states.pdf

Ackerman, C. E. (2021, April 3). Learned helplessness: Seligman's theory of depression (+ cure). Positive Psychology. https://positivepsychology.com/learned-helplessness-seligman-theory-depression-cure/

Adeney, P. (2021). Mr. Money Mustache. https://www.mrmoneymustache.com/

Allen, D. (2002). *Getting things done: The art of stress-free productivity.* Penguin Books.

Allen, D. (2012). David Allen defines "mind like water." GTD. https://gettingthingsdone.com/2012/05/david-allen-defines-mind-like-water/

Arends, B. (2020, November 3). Opinion: The inventor of the '4% rule' just changed it. Marketwatch. https://www.marketwatch.com/story/the-inventor-of-the-4-rule-just-changed-it-11603380557

Bernstein, W. J. (2009). *The investor's manifesto: Preparing for prosperity, Armageddon, and everything in between.* Wiley.

Bilanich, B. (2018). Do roses come with thorns, or do thorns come with roses? Fast Company.

Bogle, J. C. (2005, February 2). In investing, you get what you *don't* pay for. The World Money Show. http://johncbogle.com/speeches/JCB_MS0205.pdf

Botella, E. (2019, September 12). The surprising science behind why people underestimate their lifespans. Forbes. https://www.forbes.com/sites/elenabotella/2019/09/12/people-underestimate-how-long-theyll-live/?sh=2105dc563ebb

Burdick, D. (2021). The lazy river: An exercise in mindfulness. PESI. https://www.pesi.com/blog/details/846/the-lazy-river-an-exercise-in-mindfulness

Carosa, C. (2021, August 23). Covid or policy: What's causing this inflation surge? Forbes. https://www.forbes.com/sites/chriscarosa/2021/08/23/covid-or-policy-whats-causing-this-inflation-surge/?sh=ec378ff4c0fa

Clark, G. L., Feiner, A., & Viehs, M. (2015). From the stockholder to the stakeholder: How sustainability can drive financial outperformance. University of Oxford, Arabesque Partners. https://papers.ssrn.com/sol3/papers.cfm?abstract_id=2508281

Cooley, P. L., Hubbard, C. M., & Walz, D. T. (1998). Retirement savings: Choosing a withdrawal rate that is sustainable. *AAII Journal 10*(3), 16-21.

Cox, D., Hallam, R., O'Connor, K., & Rachman, S. (1983). An experimental analysis of fearlessness and courage. *British Journal of Psychology, 74*(1), 107-117.

Dickey, R. A. & Coffey, W. (2012). *Wherever I wind up: My quest for truth, authenticity, and the perfect knuckleball.* Blue Rider Press.

Dweck, C. (2007) *Mindset: The new psychology of success. How we can learn to fulfill our potential.* Ballantine Books.

Fama, E. F. (1965). Random walks in stock market prices. *Financial Analysts Journal, 21*(5), 55-59.
https://www.jstor.org/stable/4469865

Fama, E. F. & French, K. R. (1996). Multifactor Explanations of Asset Pricing Anomalies. *The Journal of Finance, 51*(1), 55-84.
https://doi.org/10.1111/j.1540-6261.1996.tb05202.x

Fenton-O'Creevy, M., Nicholson, N., Soane, E., & Willman, P. (2010). Trading on illusions: Unrealistic perceptions of control and trading performance. *Occupational and Organizational Psychology, 76*(1), 53-68. https://doi.org/10.1348/096317903321208880

Frazzini, A., Kabiller, D., and Pedersen, L. H. (2018). Buffett's alpha. *Financial Analysts Journal, 74*(4), 35-55.
https://dx.doi.org/10.2139/ssrn.3197185

French, B. (n.d.). The art of asset location.
https://retirementresearcher.com/art-asset-location/

Gardner, D. and Gardner, T. (2002, July 9). Doing hard time with Arthur Levitt [Special] July 9, 2002.
https://www.fool.com/specials/2002/07/09/foolcom-doing-hard-time-with-arthur-levi.aspx

Genworth. (2021). Cost of care survey.
https://www.genworth.com/aging-and-you/finances/cost-of-care.html

Gielan, M. (2018). Mind over money: How optimism connects to financial health. Frost.
https://www.optforoptimism.com/optimism/optimismresearch.pdf

Gielan, M. (2019). The financial upside of being an optimist. Harvard Business Review. https://hbr.org/2019/03/the-financial-upside-of-being-an-optimist

Gladwell, M. (2008). *Outliers: The story of success.* Little, Brown and Company.

Goldratt, E. (2012). *The goal: A process of ongoing improvement—30th anniversary edition.* North River Press.

Good Life Project. (2020). Anders Ericsson: Dismantling the 10,000 hour rule. Good Life Project. https://www.goodlifeproject.com/podcast/anders-ericsson/

Harris, R. (2011). *The confidence gap: A guide to overcoming fear and self-doubt.* Trumpeter.

Hayden, A. (2021, September 28). How to cut your tax bill with tax-loss harvesting. Charles Schwab. https://www.schwab.com/resource-center/insights/content/reap-benefits-tax-loss-harvesting-to-lower-your-tax-bill

James, W. (1890). *The principles of psychology.* Henry Holt and Company.

Jones, J. (2021, August 27). 5 habits to add to your day to prevent cognitive decline. https://www.eatingwell.com/article/7915302/habits-to-add-to-your-day-to-prevent-cognitive-decline/

Kahneman, D. (2011). *Thinking, fast and slow.* Farrar, Straus and Giroux.

Keller, J., Kwasnicka, D., Klaiber, P., Sichert, L., Lally, P., & Fleig, L. (2021). Habit formation following routine-based versus time-based cue planning: A randomized control trial. *British Journal of Health Psychology, 26*(3), 807-824. https://doi-org.ezproxy.bgsu.edu/10.1111/bjhp.12504

Lally, P., van Jaarsveld, C. H. M., Potts, H. W. W., & Wardle, J. (2009). How are habits formed: Modelling habit formation in the real world. *European Journal of Social Psychology, 40*(6), 998-1009. https://doi-org.ezproxy.bgsu.edu/10.1002/ejsp.674

Langer, E. J. (1975). The illusion of control. *Journal of Personality and Social Psychology, 32*(2), 311-328. https://psycnet.apa.org/doi/10.1037/0022-3514.32.2.311

Latham, G. P. (2004). The motivational benefits of goal-setting. *The Academy of Management Executive (1993-2005), 18*(4), 126-129. https://www.jstor.org/stable/4166132

Lear, S. (2020). How optimism benefits your health. Heart & Stroke. https://www.heartandstroke.ca/articles/how-optimism-benefits-your-health

Lee, L. O., James, P., Zevon, E. S., Kim, E. S., Trudel-Fitzgerald, C., Spiro III, A., Grodtein, F., & Kubzansky, L. D. (2019). Optimism is associated with exceptional longevity in 2 epidemiologic cohorts of men and women. *Proceedings of the National Academy of Sciences of the United States of America, 116*(37), 18357-18362. https://doi.org/10.1073/pnas.1900712116

Life is Good. (2018). Comprehensive study shows Americans remain optimistic in troubled times. PR Newswire. https://www.prnewswire.com/news-releases/comprehensive-study-shows-americans-remain-optimistic-in-troubled-times-300711817.html

Locke, E. A., Latham, G.P., Smith, K. J., & Wood, R. E. (1990). A theory of goal setting & task performance. Pearson College Div.

Locke, T. (2021). 3 investing lessons Warren Buffett shared at the 2021 Berkshire Hathaway meeting. CNBC Make It. https://www.cnbc.com/2021/05/03/investing-lessons-from-warren-buffett-at-berkshire-hathaway-meeting.html

Lomax, A. & Rotonti, J. (2021, August 19). What is ESG investing & what are ESG stocks? The Motley Fool. https://www.fool.com/investing/stock-market/types-of-stocks/esg-investing/

Mann, B. (2016, November 11). Educate. Amuse. Enrich. https://www.fool.com/investing/general/2008/10/15/educate-amuse-enrich.aspx

McLeod, S. (2020, December 29). Maslow's hierarchy of needs. Simply Psychology. https://www.simplypsychology.org/maslow.html

Orth, U., Trzesniewski, K. H., & Robins, R. W. (2010). Self-esteem development from young adulthood to old age: A cohort-sequential longitudinal study. *The Journal of Personality and Social Psychology, 98*(4), 645-658. https://doi-org.ezproxy.bgsu.edu/10.1037/a0018769

Pechter, K. (2019, October 10). 'Safety First' income plans, per Wade Pfau. Retirement Income Journal. https://retirementincomejournal.com/article/the-safety-first-retirement-plan-via-wade-pfau/

Pleven, L. (2013, November 28). In Bogle family, it's either passive or aggressive. The Wall Street Journal. https://www.wsj.com/articles/SB10001424052702303332904579224351143883302

Pisani, B. (2020, September 18). Stock picking has a terrible track record, and it's getting worse. CNBC: Trader Talk. https://www.cnbc.com/2020/09/18/stock-picking-has-a-terrible-track-record-and-its-getting-worse.html

PR Newswire (2010). Current issue of ai5000: Black swan author Nassim Taleb compares Buffett and Soros. https://www.prnewswire.com/news-releases/current-issue-of-ai5000-black-swan-author-nassim-taleb-compares-buffett-and-soros-83801722.html

Rotter, J. B. (1966). Generalized expectancies for internal versus external control of reinforcement. *Psychological Monographs: General and Applied (80)*1, 1-28.

Royal, J. and O'Shea, A. (2021, August 11). What is the average stock market return? NerdWallet. https://www.nerdwallet.com/article/investing/average-stock-market-return

Sauer, S. J., Rodgers, M. S., Becker, W. J. (2018). The effects of goals and pay structure on managerial reporting dishonesty. *Journal of Accounting, Ethics & Public Policy, 19*(3), 377-418.

Saunders, E. G. (2017, July 4). A way to plan if you're bad at planning. *Harvard Business Review.* https://hbr.org/2017/07/a-way-to-plan-if-youre-bad-at-planning

Sharpe, W. F. (1994). The Sharpe ratio. https://web.stanford.edu/~wfsharpe/art/sr/SR.htm

Srivastava, S., McGonigal, K., Richards, J. M., Butler, E. A., & Gross, J. J. (2006). Optimism in close relationships: How seeing things in a positive light makes them so. *Journal of Personality and Social Psychology, 91*(1). 143-153. https://psycnet.apa.org/doi/10.1037/0022-3514.91.1.143

Steinhilber, B. (2017). How to train your brain to be more optimistic. NBC News. https://www.nbcnews.com/better/health/how-train-your-brain-be-more-optimistic-ncna795231

Stich, A. (2020, May 6). The 3 types of investors, and how advisors can better serve them. ThinkAdvisor. https://www.thinkadvisor.com/2020/05/06/the-3-types-of-investors-and-how-advisors-can-better-serve-them/

Taleb, N. (2007). *The black swan: The impact of the highly improbable.* Random House Publishing Group.
Tigar, L. (2020, December 30). Why setting goals is good for you (even if you don't always meet them). Real Simple. https://www.realsimple.com/health/mind-mood/setting-goals-benefits

Tyler, N., Heffernan, R., & Fortune, C-A. (2020, September 15). Reorienting locus of control in individuals who have offended through strengths-based interventions: Personal agency and the good lives model. *Frontiers in Psychology.* https://www.frontiersin.org/articles/10.3389/fpsyg.2020.553240/full

U.S. Securities and Exchange Commission. (2018, May 29). An introduction to 529 plans. https://www.sec.gov/reportspubs/investor-publications/investorpubsintro529htm.html

US SIF. (2020, November 16). Report on US sustainable and impact investing trends. https://www.ussif.org/trends

Virginia Tech. (2018, December 11). Employee incentives can lead to unethical behavior in the workplace. ScienceDaily. Retrieved August 3, 2021, from www.sciencedaily.com/releases/2018/12/181211122456.htm

Voigt, K. (2021, May 2). Real estate vs. stocks: Which is the better investment? NerdWallet. https://www.nerdwallet.com/article/investing/real-estate-vs-stocks-which-is-the-better-investment

Wood, W. (2019). *Good habits, bad habits: The science of making positive changes that stick.* Farrar, Straus and Giroux.

Wood, W., Quinn., J. M., & Kashy, D. A. (2002). Habits in everyday life: Thought, emotion, and action. *Journal of Personality and Social Psychology, 83*(6), 1281-1297.
https://doi.org/10.1037%2F0022-3514.83.6.1281
What is a Profession?. (n.d.) What is a profession? *Australian Council of Professions.* https://www.professions.org.au/what-is-a-professional/

Young, J. R. (2020, May 5). Researcher behind '10,000-hour rule' says good teaching matters, not just practice. Edsurge.
https://www.edsurge.com/news/2020-05-05-researcher-behind-10-000-hour-rule-says-good-teaching-matters-not-just-practice

About Clark Asset Management

Clark Asset Management serves pre-retirees and retirees. We work with naturally curious, thoughtful, and savvy individuals who want to build and safeguard their wealth and support our clients in achieving a feeling of relaxed confidence in retirement.

www.Bradleyclark.com

Printed in the USA
CPSIA information can be obtained
at www.ICGtesting.com
JSHW020732071223
52795JS00004B/6/J